Readers Have Big Jobs to Do: Fluency, Phonics, and Comprehension

Lucy Calkins, Series Editor

Elizabeth Franco, Havilah Jespersen, and Lindsay Barton

Photography by Peter Cunningham

Illustrations by Elizabeth Franco

HEINEMANN ◆ PORTSMOUTH, NH

For my father, John, who showed me that life can be like learning to ride a bicycle. Sometimes there will be bumps; sometimes things will feel wobbly; but with support, you can ride off on your own. Thanks Dad, for holding on until I was ready.—Liz

For my mother, Janice, who taught me how to read, and did so with joy.—Havilah

For my parents, Peggy and Jim, who ignited my lifelong passion for reading.—Lindsay

Heinemann
361 Hanover Street
Portsmouth, NH 03801–3912
www.heinemann.com

Offices and agents throughout the world

The authors and publisher wish to thank those who have generously given permission to reprint borrowed material:

In the Days of Dinosaurs: The Dinosaur Chase, by Hugh Price. Copyright © 2013 HMH Supplement Publishers. Used by permission of Cengage Australia.

Zelda and Ivy: The Runaways. Copyright © 2006 by Laura McGee Kvasnosky. Reproduced by permission of the publisher, Candlewick Press.

From *Green Light Reader: Tumbleweed Stew*, by Susan Stevens Crummel. Illustrated by Janet Stevens. Copyright © 2000 by Houghton Mifflin. All rights reserved. Reprinted by permission of Houghton Mifflin Harcourt Publishing Company.

Frog and Toad Are Friends by Arnold Lobel . Text copyright © 1970 Arnold Lobel. Illustrations copyright © 1970 Arnold Lobel. Used by permission of HarperCollins Publishers.

Materials by Kaeden Books and Lee & Low Books, appearing throughout the primary Reading Units of Study series, are reproduced by generous permission of the publishers. A detailed list of credits is available in the Grade 1 online resources.

Cataloging-in-Publication data is on file with the Library of Congress.

ISBN-13: 978-0-325-07705-5

Series editorial team: Anna Gratz Cockerille, Karen Kawaguchi, Tracy Wells, Felicia O'Brien, Debra Doorack, Jean Lawler, Marielle Palombo, and Sue Paro
Production: Elizabeth Valway, David Stirling, and Abigail Heim
Cover and interior designs: Jenny Jensen Greenleaf
Photography: Peter Cunningham
Illustrations: Elizabeth Franco
Composition: Publishers' Design and Production Services, Inc.
Manufacturing: Steve Bernier

Printed in the United States of America on acid-free paper
22 21 20 19 18   PAH   5 6 7 8 9

Acknowledgments

WHEN LUCY CALKINS ASKS you to write a book, you want to take a second to pinch yourself and make sure it's really happening. Being invited to work as part of this immensely important project has been a privilege—one we are incredibly grateful for. At one time or another, each of us started down this path as one of Lucy's graduate students. When we think back to those first days, we doubt any of us could have even imagined working as a part of her team to author a book. And yet even then, Lucy believed in us more than we did in ourselves. She challenged us, inspired us, mentored us, and then opened doors for us, saying, "Go on—you've got this." Lucy, the words *thank you* just don't seem to be quite enough. We are better educators, writers, and, frankly, people because of you.

If you have ever had the privilege of watching Amanda Hartman teach in a classroom, then you'll understand our next acknowledgment. She has the ability to walk into a room and within seconds transform it into a learning community full of engagement, rigor, and fun. It seems positively magical. You can imagine then just how lucky we are that she was willing to sprinkle that magic on this book with her thoughtful suggestions, drawn from deep reservoirs of knowledge and experience.

It's important to also acknowledge that this work was built on the foundation of years of research, thought, and practice as a result of the incredibly talented work of the Teachers College Reading and Writing Project community. In particular, we want to thank the leadership at the Project: Laurie Pessah, Kathleen Tolan, Mary Ehrenworth, Amanda Hartman, and, of course, Lucy Calkins. We would also like to thank the incredible team of primary staff developers, especially Katie Wears and Natalie Louis, for thoughtful feedback and for being a sounding board.

In addition to the staff at the project, the teaching in this book is also built from all we have learned from other mentors in the field. In particular, Peter Johnston's work shapes so much of what we believe is important in the words we use with children, and Marie Clay's lifetime of work studying the development of young readers has had a profound impact on our work with children.

Of course, all three of us have been influenced by the mentors, teachers, colleagues, and children we've worked with throughout the years, including Angie Uyhum, Tracey DeLucia, Diane Griggs, and Jackie Jacobson from Cambridge Public Schools; and Bonnie Lebowitz and Sanaa El Hassany from Edmonton Public Schools.

An extra special thanks to all the teachers who have piloted this work, including Lisa LaForte from Crystal Lake School, Ashley Caputo from Center Elementary School, Lauren Rudd from the American School in Paris, Liz Mason from Kiel Elementary School, and Alissa Stoever from Westorchard Elementary School. We would also like to extend a thank you to Krissy Giordano and Catherine Maddox, who contributed to the initial thinking behind this unit.

Thank you to the unbelievably dedicated team at Heinemann, especially Deb Doorack, our editor. We are grateful to have had Deb's expert eye carefully combing through every word with care and precision. A special thank you to Abby Heim and her extraordinary team. We are especially grateful for the production wizardry of Elizabeth Valway, David Stirling, and Amanda Bondi, and for the marketing and sales energy of Lisa Bingen, Stephen Perepeluk, Anita Gildea, and Chuck Filo. We are overwhelmed with gratitude for the entire Heinemann team.

Finally, we'd like to acknowledge the people who have been by our side throughout this process. Writing a book takes inordinate amounts of time, persistence, and energy. We are lucky to have been supported by friends and family who endured late nights, work-filled weekends, and interrupted vacations (yes, even of the beach kind) with understanding, compassion, and a belief in the importance of our work.

—Havilah, Lindsay, and Liz

Contents

Registration instructions to access the digital resources that accompany this book may be found on p. xv.

An Orientation to the Unit

IT'S PROBABLY HARD TO BELIEVE that the children in front of you are the same children that first appeared at your classroom door in September. Back then, they looked, acted, and read so much more like kindergartners. Take a moment to think back and be proud of just how far they have come. Now think about where you're headed next. To best understand this, you may want to walk down the hall to the second-grade room and acquaint yourself with a proficient second-grade reader. They're easy to spot. They're the ones with their nose in a book, entirely lost in a story. Watch how they take charge of themselves as readers, approaching texts with confidence and enthusiasm. Talk to them and you'll discover that they draw from a deep reservoir of ways to tackle trouble, solving words and confusing parts flexibly and creatively. Listen in to the child read a page and marvel at the way it sounds. And as you talk, laugh, and wonder together, relish their enthusiasm for a great book. Now take these observations with you, all the way back to your first-grade class and use them to help you envision the foundation you'll need to build, right here and now, at this critical juncture in the lives of your readers.

It will be hard work. And so, your very first order of business in this unit will be to recruit help. "I think you're finally ready," you'll say to your class dramatically. "I think you're ready for some new and important jobs. And these aren't jobs like being a line leader or a closet monitor. Oh no. These jobs are so much bigger and more important than that. These are the jobs that *readers* do to read harder and harder books. And here's what's even more special about these reading jobs—YOU are the boss! You are in charge of your reading, *not me!*"

This unit, all about the reading process, comes at a time in the year when your readers will need to develop independence to make it to the finish line. While it's commonly accepted that kids have "made it" as first-grade readers if they reach the benchmark of reading level I/J/K texts, in reality that finish line encompasses so much more than a reading level. Instead, it's about the level of processing kids are doing in their reading and the mind-set they have about what can sometimes feel like hard work. Think back to that second-grader and what you observed. Chances are it wasn't the level of the book that stood out to you, but the way the reader took on the work of reading with joy and independence. This unit sets children up to be able to read increasingly complex texts with accuracy, comprehension, and fluency, all of which require the development of great problem-solving skills. Think of this as the book that helps you dismantle the training wheels. "Watch out for the bumps," you'll say, "but I know you can do this. Go on!"

Your main goal then, is to help your students realize that they're ready to take on the important jobs a reader needs to do. They have strategies to be in charge of their own reading, to set their own agenda, and to get through the hard parts all by themselves. They can move past the initial impulse to say "Help me!" when faced with a tricky word or when meaning breaks down and can take a deep breath, have a little courage, and say, "I can solve this myself!" You'll show your first-graders that they can be the *bosses* of their reading, solving their own reading dilemmas by drawing on the tools and strategies they've learned from minilessons and small-group work. And you'll teach them to balance their reading energies between word solving and meaning making so that their experiences with texts are well-rounded and thoughtful, efficient, and meaningful.

This is important work, worthy of teaching to your whole class, not just relegated to small-group work. There is something incredibly powerful about sharing learning as a classroom community. Think of the children who one day, in collective astonishment, witnessed a butterfly emerge from a chrysalis. "Remember?" they say to each other months later, recalling their fascinated observations. Learning together builds a sense of identity as a community. So, go ahead, tap into this as you teach about the reading process. When you meet on the carpet and teach that *all* readers read carefully, monitoring for when something doesn't make sense or doesn't match the print on the page or doesn't sound quite right, you make this the mission of the group. Now your readers belong to a community of readers that see themselves as the kind of people that watch out for problems and try to solve them. And regardless of the levels children are reading, they'll leave that carpet with a little more independence and a greater willingness to work through difficulty. It's a game changer.

In the first bend of this journey, you'll start the unit by helping your class develop the mind-set needed to take charge of their own reading. Children will learn to stop as soon as they encounter difficulty, draw from the strategies they've been accumulating all year to solve a problem, and then check to see that they've got it right. This portion of the unit is all about monitoring one's reading and initiating action. It's then in the second bend that you'll focus on strengthening and expanding students' word-solving strategies, adding more tools to their toolkits, and reminding students to draw from multiple sources of information in their problem solving. You'll review some of the work from earlier units, and now teach your readers how to use these strategies in higher-level texts, with longer, more complex words. The third bend shifts the attention toward monitoring for meaning. Children will learn strategies for maintaining meaning across large parts of text as well as strategies for developing an understanding of new vocabulary words. You'll bring the unit to a close with the fourth bend that asks your readers to pull together everything they've learned to problem solve on the run and read with fluency.

THE INTERSECTION OF READING DEVELOPMENT AND THIS UNIT

For the first time, many of your readers will be able to walk into a public library or bookstore and realize the world of text is opening up to them. All of a sudden, they'll reach for books like *Hattie and the Fox* or Little Critter, Fly Guy, or Henry and Mudge series books and be able read them. How exciting! However, like training wheels coming off a bike, things can sometimes be a little wobbly at first. New challenges arise, and it will be important to understand the work your readers need to do at this stage in their development.

First, it's critical that children learn to monitor their reading effectively. This is nothing new. Since kindergarten, your students have been taught to

check that their reading makes sense, sounds right, and looks right. After all, you can't fix up a problem if you don't know there's something wrong. With practice, and as the books they read become more challenging, kids need to get better at monitoring. At levels E/F, children are still learning to look at all the parts of a word. They may not notice that something is wrong in their reading until well past the error. At levels G/H, there is usually less distance between the error and the correction, and by level I, most readers are skilled enough at looking closely at words while still keeping in mind the meaning of the story that they will usually stop and fix up their reading at the point of error. Keep in mind, that monitoring one's reading involves both checking the accuracy of the words a reader says as well as noticing when meaning breaks down across longer parts of text. Your readers will need to know that it's their job to read with all cylinders firing, attending closely and stopping as soon as they find something wrong.

Once students realize there's a problem, then it's up to them to do something about it. To do this, readers need to have a repertoire of strategies they know how to use. The good news is that first-graders are collectors. They spread out their sports cards, their Beanie Boos, or their Pokemon cards, delighting in the number and variety they've gathered. And so in this unit, you will lean into this impulse and invite them to spread out not their baseball cards, but their reading strategies. Halfway through this first-grade year, your students will have a beginning repertoire of these strategies, and you'll reinforce the importance of remembering and drawing upon them.

All of your readers, regardless of their level, will need to think about meaning and structure when solving words, so this is why you'll start by highlighting these strategies in the unit. You'll then move to helping kids use visual information. In the beginning of the school year, you taught children to be flexible with letters and sounds. Now you will teach them to have even more flexibility in decoding. They will face tricky vowel clusters and will need to be flexible with parts of words, not just letters and sounds. But this adaptability can be challenging for first-graders. With their growing sense of "I can do this!" can come an equally strong sense of "There's only one way to do it!"—and if the one way they know doesn't work, they're stuck. Persistence, then, is important within this unit, but so is flexibility. You will need to push your first-graders to draw on their collection of strategies and try something else when their first attempt doesn't work. This means that your children will be working hard to orchestrate all the individual strategies they've learned, and to use them with more automaticity.

Comprehension also changes as children begin to read higher levels of text. Your students, many of whom are reading level G, H, and I books now, will need to think about the book in chunks or events. Because the books are longer, a child has to take several pages and put them together in order to say what's happening. A reader also has to recognize when something in the text becomes confusing and do something to fix the issue. It's likely that your first-graders do this work all the time. It's a rare first-grader who doesn't spend time asking, "Is this why . . . ?" and exclaiming, "So that means . . . !" when they've solved a mystery and puzzled out how things fit together in their lives. In books, though, your students may not think to do this as they grapple with other reading challenges. These readers will also have the added challenge of encountering a higher number of new vocabulary words. Not only will they need to put their decoding skills to the test to simply say the word, they'll also have to continue problem solving to figure out what the word might mean by using the context in the book. Again, that natural sense of inquisitiveness and curiosity will come in handy here as kids puzzle over potential word meanings and look for evidence of their thinking.

Fluency also plays an important role in your readers' development, as it requires children to use their comprehension to read with expression, check punctuation, and word solve, all at once. In order to problem solve words as they read, some children will need to learn to adjust their speed, slowing to solve a problem and then speeding up again. Readers at levels I and J will be doing much of their problem solving "on the run"; in other words, they should be able to solve multisyllabic words quickly and keep on reading with comprehension. Again, this requires children to orchestrate all that they know about reading and all that they have learned across this unit.

In this unit, as in many, partner work plays an important role. It will be important that your readers *feel* what it's like when they understand the story and are able to solve words—that they feel what it's like when their reading is going well. A partner can help them to do this, getting a sense of what it will be like to eventually do this independently. First-graders can also use their partnerships to talk more about strategies they know and strategies they want to learn more about. For that reason, this unit also includes some goal-setting work. Also, reading for an audience will give your students a fun and authentic reason to put all of their problem-solving strategies to use and to aim to read with high accuracy and strong fluency.

Finally, you'll notice that many of the conferring sections in this unit are designed to support students in strengthening their problem-solving skills.

There is a heavy emphasis on coaching conferences and guided reading groups, during which we suggest you listen in attentively as students read and coach only as needed with quick, clear prompts. We know children learn best by doing. By coaching kids with efficient problem solving you'll also be helping them get the feel of this work in their bones, setting them up to keep on doing it with complete independence.

At the end of first grade, many of your children will be reading chapter books. Right now they're on the runway, starting to pick up steam as readers, moving faster and starting to zoom along. Soon they will have to do the comprehension work of more proficient readers in longer books, and when this happens, there will be no time to also do methodical word solving. Those things have to be automatic so children's attention can be spent on meaning. This unit helps to make that transition happen.

OVERVIEW

This unit moves through four parts. The first bend strengthens readers' abilities to monitor their reading and take action when they encounter problems. The second helps readers develop efficient strategies for word solving, while the third bend helps children maintain comprehension in longer texts. The final bend invites children to put it all together and read with fluency, showing off the skills they've developed over the course of the unit.

Bend I: Readers Have Important Jobs to Do

In the first bend, children learn that they are ready to take on big and important jobs as a reader. On the very first day, the aim is to get the kids in your room to sit a little taller, hold their heads up high, and take pride in the their ability to take charge of their reading. "When readers are the boss of their own reading," you'll say with the utmost conviction, "one of the most important jobs they have is to STOP at the first sign of trouble. Then they say, 'I can solve this! I can try something, using all that I know.'" Don't underestimate the importance of this teaching. In a fascinating study of proficient second-grade readers, Elizabeth Kayne (2002) studied students' miscues to try to determine what proficient readers do when they encounter trouble. One of the most striking results, and one we use to guide our teaching at this point in first grade, was that when faced with a challenging word, *all* of those readers attempted the word independently. Not one reader skipped the challenge or stopped and stalled. In other words, proficient readers do *something* when they run into trouble. They're the kind of readers that roll up their sleeves and get to work when they see a problem.

While you will most likely recognize this trait in some of the children in your room, your goal will be to sweep everyone up into adopting this stance. Marie Clay (2005) suggested two things we can do to help passive readers change the pattern in their behavior: teach the reader to try out different responses, and have them verify the decisions they made—or in the words of this series: "Try something," and then "Check it!" Then, you'll teach your readers how to do "The Triple Check," drawing on not just one source of information but all three, by asking themselves, "Does it make sense? Does it sound right? and Does it look right?" These questions will almost become a class mantra, and you'll prompt for them over and over again until they become second nature for all your readers.

Over the course of the bend, you'll do everything you can to have all children buy in. Your goal is to help *all* your readers, even those who struggle, to act with a sense of agency, and say "I've got this! It's a problem, but I can do something about it!" And you'll want children to understand that they're not in this alone. Together, you'll make a sign that reads *"Caution! Readers at Work"* and post it outside your door for the whole school to see. And at the end of each day's workshop, you'll gather your readers together on the carpet and unveil a new verse to a lively song that celebrates the problems you've encountered, creating energy and enthusiasm for this new work. Set to the tune of "If You're Happy and You Know It," when you get to the last line of this song, you'll have every child caught up in the vision of the unit, singing out, *"When the job gets really tough, and you want to huff and puff, be the boss of your own reading, be the boss!"*

Of course, you know that simply telling a child to take charge and initiate action when in trouble won't necessarily mean this skill will automatically transfer to his or her independent reading. So making sure kids have accessible texts in hand, you'll turn to your conferences and small-group work to help students apply their learning. The important thing at this point in the unit, regardless of a child's reading level, is to coach in ways that foster independence. "Wow!" You'll say when a reader hits the brakes at a point of difficulty. "You noticed something was wrong! I can't wait to see what you're going to try!" Convey with all the enthusiasm you can muster that problems are fun to solve and that you have full confidence in every student to take

initiative. And when you observe a child solving a problem successfully, be sure to name what the child did for the rest of the class and celebrate the discoveries she made about herself as a reader. As Peter Johnston (2004) reminds us, it's up to us to weave a narrative for children in which they become central characters, ones who know how to solve problems by taking action.

As this bend wraps up, you'll invite students to reflect on all they've learned about problem solving tricky words over the last two units and evaluate their own reading habits. "Readers who are in charge make *big plans* for their reading," you'll announce. "They think, 'What do I do *a lot*? What can I do even MORE?' and they make a plan to be the best they can be." Then you'll expand on the partner work students do together by teaching children to support each other with these plans. Creating a fishbowl around a partnership, you'll highlight the ways partners can help each other when they run into big problems, not by telling a word, but by giving each other tips and cheering each other on. "This doesn't just help you solve your problem," you'll say, "It helps you learn to do your job even better every day!"

Bend II: Readers Add New Tools to Read Hard Words

In the second bend, you'll continue to build on the strategies students learned during the first two units for problem solving words. If you have many readers moving into reading texts at levels H/I/J, this work becomes especially important. Readers will encounter more multisyllabic words, a higher number of words with complex spelling patterns, and a wider range of vocabulary. In addition, by level I readers are expected to be able to solve words "on the run," with minimal interruptions to fluency.

Luckily, your children come into this unit already knowing a lot about ways to solve words. You'll start this second bend by letting them in on a little secret. "Now that you're so great at all of these jobs, you must be ready for some even bigger challenges. But here's the thing about big jobs … the tougher the job, the bigger the tool you need. If somebody is building a house, for example, that person would have little jobs and big jobs to do. For a little job, the person could just grab a shovel off the shelf. But a bigger job would need a BIGGER tool—something more powerful, like . . . a bulldozer! Are you ready to use some bigger, more powerful tools in your reading?" Then, pointing to the strategy "check the picture" (one students have been using since the first unit), you'll say, "Let's start with this tool. We need to make this tool as big as a bulldozer!" You'll then demonstrate for kids how the picture doesn't necessarily help problem solve words in more a complex text. Instead, you'll teach your readers to still draw from meaning as a source of information, but to do so by thinking about what's happening and synthesizing information across the text.

In this way, each session of this bend either introduces students to a new tool for solving words or lifts the level of an old tool. As you work through this bend, you'll revise and build upon the word-solving chart. You might even make this chart look like a toolkit and let kids know that by the end of the bend it will be bursting at the seams with strategies they can try. Throughout this bend you'll teach strategies to support students in using each of the sources of information: you'll start with a lesson each on meaning and structure, before devoting the rest of the bend to visual strategies. There's a reason why meaning and structure are placed up front in the unit—these are critical, and as you shift to a focus on visual information, you'll want to make sure kids are still using meaning and structure in every problem they solve. Likewise, even though a session may highlight a particular strategy, you'll notice a deliberate attempt to model the integration of meaning, structure, and visual information in each day's teaching.

If you take the time to observe proficient readers using visual information in their problem solving, there are some valuable lessons to take away. Strong readers are remarkably efficient and flexible in their ability to decode words. In the same study of proficient readers referenced earlier, Kayne (2002) found that the students demonstrated more than 60 different ways of solving words and that almost all of these involved using word parts. It makes sense. It's the fastest way to use visual information when figuring out a word, and that means you can get on with reading a great book!

But in order to work with such efficiency, readers have to know a lot about the way words work and must be able to apply this knowledge within texts. The remaining sessions in the second bend support children in doing this. You'll start by showing readers how to break words in a variety of ways. Comparing words to Lego® blocks, you'll describe a time you saw a Lego castle and didn't think you could ever build something as hard as that, until you learned that it was just built part-by-part. You'll say, "I was so busy looking at the *whole* castle that I didn't think about the smaller parts. I could build walls and then add the towers and then add the bridge. Then at the end, I could step back, look at it all together and realize that I had built an amazing castle too." You'll show your readers that the same principle applies to words, as you say, "You might think, 'Whoa! I can't read a word like THAT!' But remember,

it's not that hard. You just have to read it part-by-part!" Then, using magnetic letters to make the concept three dimensional, you'll recruit kids to work with you to break words in a variety of ways: breaking a word from its inflectional ending, breaking an onset from a rime, and breaking a word apart by syllables.

Your readers will also be taught to draw on what they have learned in word study about spelling patterns, drawing on sight words in text, and using a strategy called analogy (using a word you know, such as *make*, to read an unknown word like *bakery*). Throughout the lessons you'll notice an attempt to cultivate a sense of curiosity about words. Just like in the last unit, where you helped to carry students' natural curiosity about the world into their reading, you'll teach them to bring this same excitement to investigating how words work and using that knowledge to figure out the tricky ones. When teaching readers to try different letter sounds you'll create a chart called "Caught You! Sneaky Sounds in Our Books," inviting readers to watch out for sneaky sounds and study them closely. And when using analogy, students will discover the "magic" of knowing that one word can help them read lots of words. "Alacazam!" you'll say as you turn *hat* into *splat* and *stop* into *stand*.

There are a few underlying principles that span these word-solving sessions. First, the sessions provide the opportunity for lots of repeated practice in context, prompting children to return to texts to show how each strategy transfers to the books they read. In addition, we have been influenced by the work of Marie Clay, so you will notice a deliberate attempt to scaffold the learning so that children usually try out a strategy on a word they know before applying it to an unknown word. Because reading and writing are reciprocal processes, children will also have opportunities to apply word-solving strategies as both a writer and a reader. Lastly, this bend emphasizes the importance of flexibility. You will ask your readers to try solving a word one way and then another, encouraging them to take a tentative stance as they learn more about words and the ways they work.

Bend III: Readers Add Tools to *Understand* Their Books

In the third bend, the focus of your teaching will shift back to meaning. It's important that your readers understand that all of the work they've been doing to become stronger at solving words serves a bigger purpose—to help them better understand their books! When children devote their attention to word solving, they sometimes unintentionally let go of meaning. In addition, as they begin to read longer and more complex texts, it becomes increasingly challenging to keep track of what's happening in those books. The primary goal for this bend, then, is to help your readers monitor for meaning.

You'll make this clear from the very start of the bend by saying, "Figuring out the words is only *one* of your jobs as a reader. Readers actually have a way *bigger* and more *important* job to do. Readers must *always*—*every* time they read—work hard to *understand* their books." You'll practice this by reading the next section of your demonstration text, pausing every so often to have students do a quick check for comprehension and recap what they know so far. Your readers will learn that just like when they run into trouble on a word, they can *stop* and *do something*, such as rereading to clarify, when comprehension becomes a problem.

To give students ample opportunity for practice, you'll tap into the fun of drama by teaching partnerships to act as news reporters. "This just in!" you'll announce, holding an imaginary microphone in one hand and clasping an earpiece with the other. "We have an update on Zelda and Ivy's time capsule. Ivy just snuck over to the cherry tree and dug up the time capsule. But when she looked inside, she saw only her doll, Mimi!" You'll then extend this retelling by showing your readers how a strong understanding of the text also helps readers to make predictions. "We know from going back and checking the facts that two objects were put into the time capsule!" you'll say, continuing in your role as a news reporter. "This is very strange! Partner 2, what do you think is going to happen *next*?" As your room fills with news reporters, students will be working together to reread, ask questions, make predictions, and talk about their texts—work that is critical to the development of strong comprehension.

The rest of the bend responds to the new demands of level H/I/J texts: less supportive illustrations, more complex dialogue, and lots of new vocabulary words. You'll first teach children that there is so much more to a story than what an illustrator is able to capture in a picture. "Wait!" you'll say, directing kids to study the text closely. "The picture doesn't show everything that's happening. It doesn't show Ivy sighing or adding Princess Mimi to the box or Zelda digging the hole for the time capsule. I've got some work to do to make the movie in my mind show the whole scene. Okay, ready? Lights, camera, *action*!" By drawing from both the picture and the text, you will teach your readers to envision the story and bring it to life. Comparing a reader to a movie director, you'll say, "You can be a director every time you read your books, using your imagination to turn the pictures and the words on the page into a movie in your mind. That way, you'll understand what's happening even better." You'll then go on to show your readers how envisioning can help them

understand the conversations characters have in books, keeping track of who is talking and how they might be speaking. This will be important work to do now, developing a strong foundation for when your students go on to read chapter books.

Finally, you'll extend the vocabulary work children did in Unit 2, showing your readers that they can learn new words in *all* the books they read. Students will learn that taking charge of their reading means not only figuring out how to say a word but also figuring out what it might mean. You'll demonstrate how fun this work can be, coming up with one idea and then another, reading on to gather more clues. "Once you figure out what a word means," you'll say, "it's yours forever. You can use that word whenever you want, but especially when you talk about your book." Partners will then work together to mark new words and discuss them, trading words "just like you might trade bracelets or baseball cards."

Bend IV: Readers Use Everything They Know to Get the Job Done

In the fourth bend, you'll focus on orchestration, calling on students to pull together everything they have learned in this unit and to do so quickly. To celebrate all the hard work students have done and to provide your readers with an authentic purpose for problem solving on the run, maintaining meaning and reading fluently, you'll end the unit by having your readers create audiobooks. "Quick! Quick! I have something important to tell you about!" you'll say as set them up to begin this work. "You won't believe the advertisement I stumbled across in the morning paper!" Then read the job posting:

> WANTED: Kindergarten classrooms in desperate need of more audiobooks. The kindergartners have listened to every recording of a book in the whole school. Calling on expert readers who can make new audiobooks for the listening centers. Help please!

Your readers will be sure to volunteer for this job. To do their very best work, your class will conduct an inquiry, investigating an audiobook reading to discover what an "audiobook reading star" does to make their reading sound great. Students will then work with partners to apply these same techniques to their own reading, giving each other feedback on their fluency. On the last day of the unit you'll invite a kindergarten class to visit. Your readers will show off all they've learned by reading to a buddy, and then together you'll present the visiting class with a collection of new audiobooks. Your readers will finish the unit full of agency, proud of the work they have done, ready to tackle new challenges and armed with a host of strategies for the demands ahead.

ASSESSMENT

Study running records of your students reading instructional-level texts to learn what they do when they encounter challenges.

Running records are the most important assessment resource for this unit. Before you begin teaching, we recommend you study your students' most recent running records to refresh your memory of where they are as readers. At this point in the year, your readers should be reading level G/H texts independently. We recommend you pay particular attention to the processing students are doing in their reading. Note that if you are looking at students' running records at their independent reading levels, this information will be difficult to find. This unit is all about helping students handle challenges. Therefore you will need to look at what children do in their reading when faced with a challenge. You'll need to study what children do when they are reading at an instructional level—or even a frustration level—to discover this information. A running record without miscues leaves you nothing to study!

As you read running records, ask yourself:

- What are my students doing when they encounter trouble?
- Do they make attempts?
- Do they check their attempts?
- Do they make multiple attempts?
- What sources of information do they use?
- Do they use meaning, structure, and visual information equally, or do they lean more heavily on one information source?
- How effectively do they use sources of information?

For example, you may notice that a child often uses visual information, but attends only to the beginning of words. Although she clearly is using visual information, she is not yet using it effectively. As you study the data, you will be looking for patterns in individual children's reading as well as across your whole class. This will help you to set up some initial small groups, as well as shape the teaching you will do in this unit.

Throughout the unit you'll want to continue to collect running records on a regular basis. This can seem overwhelming, but it does not have to be. Remember, you only need to study what a child is doing on a portion of the text (usually 100–150 words), and you can take a running record of a child reading any text. These will be an invaluable source of information as you work to teach in a way that is responsive to your students' needs. To learn more about these assessments you can go to the assessment chapter in the book, *A Guide to the Reading Workshop, Primary Grades.*

Analyze other assessments to develop a comprehensive view of your readers.

You can also glean important insights from your spelling assessments or simply from studying children's writing to see how they are making sense of words and of how word parts work. For example, you might notice if a child is working through a word part by part or letter by letter. You will also be able to identify the letters, sounds, and word patterns a student knows. Look for patterns across reading, writing, and spelling assessments. If a child has difficulty with word endings, do you notice this in all three areas? A high-frequency word assessment will also be useful in helping you understand which words have become sight words for children. As readers progress through higher levels of text, they will need to expand this bank of words, both to improve their fluency and so that they have it to draw from when solving unknown words. You'll want to use the information from all of these assessments to help you decide what to focus on in small-group work across the unit. This kind of assessment-driven instruction is integral to the goal of continually moving readers toward grade-level complex texts. For more information about additional assessments you can also refer to the guide book.

Develop targeted, strategic instruction for readers who are below benchmark.

While you'll of course need to collect up-to-date information on all your readers, it's particularly important to do this often for your students reading below benchmark. Take running records on these students frequently, quickly collecting data during conferences and small groups. Make sure to carefully analyze these records, searching for patterns of both strengths and weakness. The better you know these readers (and really all your readers), the better able you'll be to target your instruction precisely. You'll turn this careful eye toward these students' other assessments as well, noting their growing bank of sight words as well as the word study patterns they control in isolation as well when solving words in context. As you begin to set up small groups across the unit, think about when you'll meet with these children and what kind of instruction you'll provide. In the Conferring and Small-Group sections throughout this unit, you'll find suggestions to target struggling students. You can also refer to the chapter on differentiation in the guide book for help. Ideally, you can draw on the support of a school reading specialist or literacy coach to help administer assessments and devise plans for each at-risk reader. Certainly, if a student is receiving additional help outside of your classroom, you will need to be sure that help is coordinated with the instruction the child receives in your class.

Use assessment data to tailor your curriculum to student needs.

As you look across your running records, conferring notes, and other sources of data, you may find that a group of your first-graders is still reading at level E, F, or G. If this is the case, you may want to refer to *If . . . Then . . . Curriculum: Assessment-Based Instruction, Grades K–2* as a resource. The unit "Word Detectives Use All They Know to Solve Words" can serve as a supplement to this unit, providing extra practice with word solving. You might decide to teach that unit in its entirety before you teach this unit, or you might select particular bends from that unit to serve as extensions, targeted to your students' needs.

GETTING READY

Gather a variety of high-interest books that span your students' current just-right levels.

Book choice is key during this unit. The focus on building strong reading behaviors that move students toward texts of greater difficulty will require lots of reading. Before the unit begins, take a moment to look over your classroom library. You'll probably find that as students move up levels there are some baskets you can put away, and new baskets, at higher levels, you can now display. Make sure you have enough books to cover the range of levels your children are reading. Your readers will need to have enough texts to last for a week of reading. Ideally, most students should be able to select between eight and twelve books a week.

To ensure children read with volume and stamina and have ample opportunity to practice what they are learning in both fiction and nonfiction books, you'll encourage students to shop across genres throughout the unit. To do so, you'll need to make sure your library is brimming with enticing nonfiction and fiction texts.

Select and gather books and texts for minilessons and guided reading.

You will want to gather up some texts to use in your minilessons. We suggest selecting demonstration texts that are a little higher than the level at which most of your students are reading. This way you'll have plenty of places to model word solving and monitoring for meaning. You can also incorporate texts that you have read together in shared-reading sessions or during read-aloud. Of course, you'll want to make sure that these are engaging texts your students enjoy.

In addition to the exemplar texts in the shared-reading and read-aloud portions of this book, we suggest *The Dinosaur Chase* (Level I). by Hugh Price (Houghton Mifflin Harcourt, 2002) and *Zelda and Ivy: The Runaways* (Level J), by Laura McGee Kvasnosky (Candlewick Press, 2013). *The Dinosaur Chase* is a quick, engaging read, likely to be close to the instructional level of many of your students and perfect for coaching students to take charge of their own reading. Your readers will no doubt identify with Little Dinosaur who also tries something and then something else to persevere and solve a very big problem.

Zelda and Ivy: The Runaways introduces children to an episodic chapter book. These two mischievous fox sisters will have students laughing along as you use this book to coach your students in using various word-solving and comprehension strategies. Using texts with this level of complexity will help make your minilessons more multileveled and will help you to address the range of needs you have in your classroom. You'll probably find that most books you use as demonstration texts will also be a good fit for additional shared reading.

Because the unit focuses on students' ability to solve problems, it's critical that children are reading books that present some challenges. You'll want to make sure you're doing lots of small-group work with instructional-level texts and then adding these books to students' book baggies so they'll have the opportunity to reread these books independently. You'll need to refer to your running records to make sure you have multiple copies of texts at students' instructional levels available for small-group work.

Create and prepare to distribute special tools.

Throughout this unit you'll want to continue to use tools that are already an integral part of your workshop time, such as book baggies and reading mats. For this unit, you'll also set up a few other basic tools. Early in the unit, you'll make (or have the children make) reading signs. They'll use these with partners, coaching each other to stop, try something, and then check it! These might also serve as bookmarks readers can use independently. Another important tool will be small versions of your anchor charts to distribute to children. You'll find copies of these in the digital resources, or you may decide to make your own. As children learn to take charge of their reading, you'll want them be involved in noticing what they do all the time and what they could do more, learning to set their own goals and then working furiously to achieve them. These mini-charts will function almost like checklists, reminding students of strategies to try and helping them take ownership of their own learning.

Think ahead toward technology you might use to create audiobooks for a final celebration.

In the final bend of this unit you'll support students in creating their own audiobooks to share with others. We recommend planning ahead for this. You might use tablets, computers, or even a phone to record students. Most of these technologies have a simple voice recording application that you (and the students) will likely find easy to use. Some teachers have enjoyed turning these audio files into QR codes and affixing them to book backs. This way, children can simply scan the QR code to play the audio recording, immediately transforming the text into an audiobook! Of course, if access to technology is a concern, you can always alter this celebration and have your readers prepare to read aloud to their kindergarten buddies.

Gather and prepare charts to support the work of this unit.

From the start of the unit you'll find yourself referencing the "Good Habits for Solving Hard Words" and "Reading Partners Work Together" charts from Units 1 and 2, so make sure they are front and center. As you move through this unit, you'll revise these charts. You'll remove strategies and behaviors your students know by heart, and you'll add new ones as their learning grows. You'll reorganize all this information to make it easy to understand.

This is also a useful time to evaluate other charts that are currently posted on your walls. By this time in the year, it's easy to get lost in a sea of chart clutter. Look around the walls, asking yourself which charts represent concepts children have mastered, which represent concepts only *some* children need, and which are still key anchors for everyone. Celebrate with the children when you take down any chart they no longer need to reference. You might make mini versions of charts that represent strategies that only some students need and have them on hand as a resource. Assessing your charts allows you to differentiate the needs of your class and frees up valuable wall space for the new learning to come.

READ-ALOUD AND SHARED READING

Use the read-aloud plan in the back of this book to help you prepare for one read-aloud across a couple of days, as well as others across the unit.

For this unit, we selected *Frog and Toad Are Friends*, by Arnold Lobel, as the read-aloud text. At the back of this book, you will find a read-aloud section where we have written a script for think-alouds, listening prompts, and turn-and-talks that you may want to do with your students. You will also see that in your kit you have little Post-it notes that have the prompts written on them, which you can directly transfer into your own copy of the book. We hope that this will help cut back on your planning time, giving you more time to study and think about your students' work. We imagine that you will then be able to take out these Post-it notes and use them in other read-aloud texts that you select. All of the prompts are transferable across texts.

Select books that are engaging and have complex stories that will be fun to talk and think about.

We chose *Frog and Toad Are Friends* as this unit's read-aloud text for several reasons. For starters, as a beloved and well-known series, Frog and Toad books are easy to find and lovely to share with children. Lobel's rich and nuanced characters are entrancing, and you probably have your own worn copy that you pulled off the shelf year after year. You'll find your kids have lots to say about these stories. Furthermore, as an episodic chapter book featuring a series of loosely connected chapters, *Frog and Toad Are Friends* is exactly the kind of book many of your readers are headed toward in the coming weeks and months. Over the course of a multi-day read-aloud, you'll support children with comprehending these longer books, guiding them through the work of Bend III. You'll help children to monitor for meaning, envision the text, follow more complicated dialogue, and infer the meaning of new vocabulary words. Your students will also hold grand conversations about their books, debating questions like "Are Frog and Toad *always* there for each other?" Before long you'll find many kids in your class digging into this classic series, ready with the thinking skills to carry them forward.

Across the unit you'll choose several other chapter books to read with children, perhaps even another book in the Frog and Toad series. In addition to these texts, you might also choose some high-quality picture books that provide lots of room for discussion and thinking. Reading books with similar themes can encourage children to think across texts. For example, you might pair Frog and Toad with a few picture books about friendship, such as *A Visitor for Bear, George and Martha,* or *Chester's Way.* You might also choose to include some nonfiction read-alouds in this unit so that children continue the comprehension skills they developed in the previous unit.

Use the five-day plan in the back of this book to help you prepare for shared reading.

Along with the read-aloud plan in the back of the book, you will find a five-day plan for shared reading. We chose to develop a plan for *Tumbleweed Stew* (Level J), by Susan Stevens Crummel. This plan is meant to be a template for how you can echo the teaching in this unit of study across a few days. Our hope is that you use this template to replicate the teaching with several other shared-reading texts that you select for the remaining weeks of your unit.

Select books for shared reading that will teach the main skills that echo your unit of study and are what your students need as readers.

We selected *Tumbleweed Stew* for several reasons. One reason we chose this book was to expose children to many different types of text. In *Tumbleweed Stew,* which is a version of the classic *Stone Soup,* Jack Rabbit sneaks under the gate into Two Circle Ranch, winning over the skeptical residents with

his excellent tumbleweed stew. Through this story, children have a chance to discover a classic folktale, either for the first time or in a new way. The book also has a beautiful cadence and rhythm, making it a perfect candidate for choral reading. It also offers plenty of opportunity for students to acquire some new vocabulary (such as *tumbleweed*). As a level J text, it is likely a notch above the reading level of many of your students and provides opportunities for guided practice with the word-solving, comprehension, and fluency work of the unit. Its short length makes it all the more accessible for students reading below this level.

☙ ONLINE DIGITAL RESOURCES

A variety of resources to accompany this and the other Grade 1 Units of Study for Teaching Reading are available in the Online Resources, including charts and examples of student work shown throughout *Readers Have Big Jobs to Do,* as well as links to other electronic resources. Offering daily support for your teaching, these materials will help you provide a structured learning environment that fosters independence and self-direction.

To access and download all the digital resources for the Grade 1 Units of Study for Teaching Reading:

1. Go to **www.heinemann.com** and click the link in the upper right to log in. (If you do not have an account yet, you will need to create one.)
2. **Enter the following registration code** in the box to register your product: RUOS_Gr1
3. Under **My Online Resources**, click the link for the ***Grade 1 Reading Units of Study***.
4. The digital resources are available under the headings; click a file name to download.

(You may keep copies of these resources on up to six of your own computers or devices. By downloading the files you acknowledge that they are for your individual or classroom use and that neither the resources nor the product code will be distributed or shared.)

You Be the Boss! Readers Say, "I Can Do This!"

IN THIS SESSION, you'll teach students that when readers take charge of their reading, they stop at the first sign of trouble and then try something to solve the problem.

GETTING READY

✔ Choose a demonstration text at, or slightly above, the current benchmark level to use across Bend I. We use *The Dinosaur Chase*, by Hugh Price (level I). You'll want to look for one that provides an engaging story and opportunities for word-solving work because you'll carry this text across subsequent lessons. You may choose a big book or use a document camera to project the text during demonstrations (see Teaching and Active Engagement).

✔ Prepare the beginning of the anchor chart for this bend by adding the heading "Be the Boss of Your Reading!" to a blank piece of chart paper. The anchor chart you'll start today will carry across the unit (see Connection).

✔ Make sure you have today's strategy Post-it® notes—"STOP at the first sign of trouble!" and "Try SOMETHING!"—ready to add to the chart (see Connection).

✔ Display the "Good Habits for Solving Hard Words" anchor chart from Units 1 and 2 (see Teaching and Active Engagement).

✔ Use a Post-it to mask a word in your demonstration text. We suggest *hole* on page 2 of *The Dinosaur Chase* (see Teaching and Active Engagement).

✔ Prepare a reading sign for each child to use in independent and partner reading. One side will say, "Stop! Try Something!" and the other will say, "Go! Keep on Reading!" (see Transition to Partner Time).

✔ Prepare a chart with the lyrics to the song "Be a Reading Boss!," which is sung to the familiar tune of "If You're Happy and You Know It." This easy-to-remember song will remind your students of what to do when they encounter trouble in their reading (see Share).

MINILESSON

CONNECTION

Rally kids around the mind-set that reading tricky words is hard work, but they can be the boss and take charge of their own reading.

"It's a brand-new unit, readers—the perfect time to take on some brand-new challenges! After all, you've been doing so much important reading work already. You have good habits when you read *and* you know so many ways to learn all about the world from your books." I leaned in dramatically. "I think you're finally ready." Then, I paused as the kids stared back at me with anticipation. "I think you're ready for some new and important jobs."

"Like the line leader?" Parker called out, pointing to the "Jobs" chart.

"And the closet monitor?" Steven added.

I laughed. "Those are jobs we have in our classroom. Just like you do important jobs to help the class, readers do important jobs to read harder and harder books. And here's what's even more special about those reading jobs: *you* are the boss! You're in charge of your reading, *not me*!" The students smiled with big-kid pride.

"So—hands up—who is ready to get to work?" Hands shot up high. "Excellent!"

❖ **Name the teaching point.**

"Today I want to teach you that when readers are the boss of their reading, one of their jobs is to *stop* at the first sign of trouble. Then they say, 'I can solve this! I can try something, using all that I know.'"

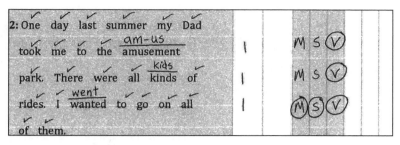

FIG. 1–1 In this record, the student continues to read straight through her errors, not stopping to problem-solve a word or self-correct a miscue. Be on the lookout for readers like this!

Start the chart.

ANCHOR CHART

Be the Boss of Your Reading!

1. STOP at the first sign of trouble!
2. Try SOMETHING!

TEACHING AND ACTIVE ENGAGEMENT

Remind readers to take a sneak peek before they read.

"Let's get to work, readers! I know you can take charge and solve any trouble you have with tough words in this book." I placed *The Dinosaur Chase* under the document camera. "I found this book in our library. It's called *The Dinosaur Chase*. Hmm, . . . because you know exactly what to do before we start a book, I'm sure you're all thinking, 'Don't just jump into reading! Take a sneak peek!'" I shook my head in admiration. "You are *so* ready to be the boss. Okay, let's do that together. That way, we'll be extra ready to find and solve any trouble in our way." I did a quick sneak peek before we moved to the work of reading the words.

If you watch your strongest readers closely, you'll probably notice that these students usually approach problems with a sense of confidence. Your goal here is to help all your readers take on this mind-set, acting with a sense of agency, saying "I've got this! It's a problem, but I can do something about it!"

Demonstrate how readers don't back down from a challenging word in their books, but instead they stop and try something, using all they know about solving words.

"Readers, your minds are *already* working hard to figure out how this story might go. Let's use all that we know to solve any trouble—like tough words—that we come across as we read." I turned to page 2 of the book and read aloud the first part, stopping at the covered word.

> *One day,*
>
> *Big Dinosaur chased Little Dinosaur*
>
> *into a _ _ _ _.*

"Oh drat! I'm in trouble already!" I slumped in my seat and crossed my arms in defeat. "This feels like it's going to get hard. I think I'm just going to skip it. Who cares?"

Then I bolted up to show I had a job to do. "Wait a minute. If I'm going to be in charge of my reading, I can't just skip the word! I need to . . ." I left some silence and pointed to our new chart.

"Stop!" a group of kids called out.

"Stop? Okay. Thanks. I'm going to have to stop and . . ." Again, I pointed to the chart.

"Try something!" a chorus of kids called back.

"Wow. You are getting bossy!" I put a hand on my hip. "You know *exactly* what to do. I'm glad I have you to help me out. Okay. You're right. I *can* do it." I took a deep breath and put my finger under the masked word. "I need to try something I already know. Hmm, . . . what do I *already* know that can help me here?"

I looked toward the class as the students began to raise their hands to help. "Can you remind me of *all* the things you already know how to do when there's a tough word in your book? Then, maybe I can try some of those strategies to help me solve this word. Make a list across your fingers."

I prompted the class to turn and talk as I leaned in to collect suggestions, quickly assessing students' repertoire for word solving.

After a moment, I called the class's attention back. "I heard so many of you sharing the good habits you have for getting unstuck in your books. I even noticed some of you looking at our word-solving chart to help you remember." I stood beside the "Good Habits for Solving Hard Words" chart from Unit 2, *Learning About the World*, to review students' repertoire. Many of you reminded me to check the picture *and* get a running start *and* look at all the parts of the word.

There are actually two big "jobs" you are asking kids to do. The first is to notice a problem. The second is to solve it. Don't underestimate the importance of the first step. Kids need to know that this is a big deal. By modeling the way you stop at a problem and do something about it, you give kids permission to find errors or acknowledge difficulty in their own reading. In fact, you are celebrating when they do so!

By inviting children to direct you in this work, you reinforce the theme of the bend, that children are independent problem solvers. It isn't enough to simply tell children that they are the "boss" of their reading; you must give them ample opportunities to assume this role.

By referring to the word-solving chart from the last unit, you are holding readers accountable for using their previous learning. You'll want to show your students that the strategies they are learning can be used in all the reading they do—across units, and across subjects throughout a day.

Good Habits for Solving Hard Words

- Check the picture.
- Look at ALL the parts of the word.
- Get a running start.
- Check it! Do a double-check!
- Try it 2 ways!
- Crash the parts together.
- Do a slow check!
- Say the word the best you can. Think about what it means.

You sure know a lot about solving hard words, and you're definitely not going to back down at the first sign of trouble. Let me try out some of your ideas here." I turned back to the book, rereading the first part:

One day,

Big Dinosaur chased Little Dinosaur

into a _ _ _ _.

"What's happening right now? Let's check the picture. Thumbs up when you've got some ideas, readers."

I gave the class a few moments to think. Then, I continued. "So Big Dinosaur is sitting up on this rock because he already chased Little Dinosaur into something." I tapped the details in the picture. "I need more clues to solve this. What else could I try?" I thought aloud, pausing to give the students a chance to chime in and suggest other ideas.

One day,
Big Dinosaur chased Little Dinosaur
into a [   ]

Big Dinosaur was very hungry.
He sat and waited
for Little Dinosaur to come out.

"Oh, maybe it's a snap word." I lifted the Post-it covering the word and scratched my head. "It's *not* a snap word." Now the students were calling out strategies on their own. "Wait, I can make the beginning sounds." I put my finger under the first part of the word, "Ho." I slid my finger under the word. "Ho-le. Hole! Let me reread and put it together to make sure it makes sense *and* sounds right." I reread to check.

One day,

Big Dinosaur chased Little Dinosaur

into a hole in a rock.

"Yes, that's it! Wow-ee! With your help, I got it. Thanks for taking charge and reminding me to *stop* and try something. I know you'll take charge of your own reading, too."

Prompt readers to transfer this same work to their own books.

"Take out one of the new books from your baggie that you brought with you and right now, get started reading that book. Don't wait for me to tell you what to do. Remember, *you're* the boss. You already know what to do before you read, and you know lots of strategies when you get stuck on hard words. Don't forget to *stop* at the first sign of trouble. Don't back down. Use all that you know to solve it! Ready, bosses?"

I moved around the meeting area, observing behaviors, on the lookout for students who remembered to take a sneak peek first, and listening to others read aloud. I coached any readers who got stuck on words, prompting them to pull from their repertoire of word-solving strategies. I voiced over reminders to individual kids so the whole group could hear: "Uh-oh! Remember to stop at the trouble!" "What can you try to help yourself here? Try something!" "You caught your mistake. Now you can fix it! I know you can do it!"

LINK

Recap the word-solving work students did and reference the "Be the Boss of Your Reading!" chart. Tell them they are hired. They are the boss of their reading.

I called students back after a minute or so. "You are most definitely hired for the job, readers! You are pushing yourself to take charge, to *stop* and try something to solve the trouble. Remember, starting right now, you are the boss of your reading, and you can help yourself read harder and harder books."

Coach the children who have difficulty noticing their errors. Instead of showing the child the mistake they made, you might gently say "Uh-oh. Something isn't right, is it? Which part needs to be fixed up?" In this way, you still leave the work for the child to do, prompting them to reread, and try to locate the error.

FIG. 1–2   To celebrate students taking charge of their reading, a teacher made them name labels.

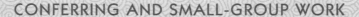

Noting and Celebrating Signs of Perseverance

Create a buzz around the new unit, rallying kids to take charge of their reading.

Your primary goal today and over the course of this first bend is to ensure that you do everything in your power to help children assume the identity of readers who are not afraid of tackling challenges independently. As you move quickly from student to student, celebrate even the smallest signs of perseverance. When you notice a child monitoring her reading and stopping at the point of error, make a big deal of this. You might say, "There are other kids who would just mumble past that tricky word, but *you* stopped. Wow. You're the kind of reader who takes charge of your reading. I can't wait to see what you do next. What are you going to try?" It may well be that this is a struggling reader who has a tendency to stop and get stuck or ask for help. With this interaction, you reinforce the child's ability to notice an error, while communicating that you fully expect this reader to take action independently.

MID-WORKSHOP TEACHING **Stop When You're Stuck *and* When Something Doesn't Seem Right!**

"I love seeing you guys reading up a storm. How many of you have already read through a bunch of books on your reading mat?" Hands shot up. "Fabulous. There is one thing I *especially* admire. I saw a lot of you not just reading, reading, reading, but also doing this." I role-played reading, slowing down, and stopping to say, "Wait! Something's not right. I need to fix this.

"Now you might wonder, 'What's the big deal?' Well, it is a *giant* deal for you to be reading along and to slow down and *stop*, not just when you can't read a word, but *anytime* you think, 'Hmm, . . . something isn't right.' When you notice that something is off, you can use your fix-up muscles to do important reading work. After all, that's *your* job!"

As you listen to children reading, you'll notice places where a child makes a miscue and then keeps on reading. This is likely because they do not yet realize they've made an error. Resist the temptation to jump in right away and point this out. Given the opportunity, as they read on, they'll likely notice something is wrong. Then praise the observation! You might say "What careful reading! Why did you stop? What did you notice?"

As you support children with solving words, you may also find that there are times when you need to tell a child a word. First, ensure the reader has had ample opportunity to solve the problem independently by suggesting strategies to try. Keep in mind you will want to make sure the child doesn't struggle so much that they become frustrated. You'll also want to make sure that meaningful reading isn't being interrupted for too long. Then, instead of simply telling the reader the word, try using the phrase, "Could it be_____?" and insert the correct word from the text. In this way, you still require the child to initiate some action. They will have to consider your suggestion, check the text, and decide if it's right—all work that helps them practice monitoring their reading. Then celebrate the approximations the child made.

When you notice a reader making multiple attempts to solve a word independently, you might also stop a whole table to draw attention to the work this child did and encourage others to do the same. Don't underestimate the power of your words. With these little compliments, you create a narrative for the community in your classroom, sending the message that even though you all run into trouble from time to time, you are the kind of readers who roll up their sleeves and have fun working hard to solve problems.

Conduct several quick table conferences to remind kids to draw on all they have learned across the year.

You'll also want to move quickly from table to table, conducting quick conferences to reinforce previous learning—naming one thing a reader is remembering to do, inviting

(continues)

"Readers, today you and your partner will each get a reading sign that you can use when you read alone, and especially when you read together. You can listen to your partner read, and if something doesn't feel quite right, or if you sense trouble, hold up this side of the sign." I revealed a sign that read, "Stop! Try something!" Then I continued. "And when your partner reads the words correctly, hold up this side of the sign." I flipped the sign, revealing the side that read, "Go! Keep on reading!"

"Ready to give it a try?" The class nodded enthusiastically. I quickly passed out a sign to each student.

FIG. 1–3   Reading signs

the rest of the table to try it, coaching each child, and then moving on. You might also choose to name strategies children are forgetting to use. For example, you might say, "I notice you're taking a sneak peek by looking at the cover, but you can also peek inside at a few of the pages to get your mind warmed up. Can you try to take a longer sneak peek to get more information about the book? Try it, and I will help you."

These conferences are meant to be quick. You might even want to carry a timer with you, to pace yourself and keep conferences tight. Research quickly by observing students' behaviors and listening to them read a bit aloud, or by asking a couple of key questions about skills from the previous unit. You might even use a small copy of all the anchor charts from the other units as a reminder of the work students should continue to do in this new unit.

Singing a Song to Remember to Stop

Teach children new lyrics to a familiar song to serve as a reminder of what do when something in their reading isn't right. Invite them to sing the song with you.

"Can I teach you a song that can help you remember this important job you have as a reader? It goes to the tune of 'If You're Happy and You Know It.' How many of you know *that* song?" A bunch of the children indicated that they did, some singing the beginning of a verse. "Great! Let's change the words to make the song about what readers have to do when something they read isn't quite right. It goes like this." I uncovered the lyrics on a piece of chart paper and sang the first line:

Be a Reading Boss!
If you think something's wrong, you've got to STOP!

I clapped my hands twice to the beat. "Now sing along with me from the top." I slid my finger across each line, singing and clapping along with the class.

Tell children that they can sing this song to themselves as they read and detect trouble. They are in charge of their own reading.

"So, readers, when you're reading on your own (or even with your partner), you can sing this song to yourself to remember that anytime you think something's wrong, you've got to . . ."

"Stop!" the kids shouted back.

"Yes! That's right. That's an important job, and *you* are the boss of your reading. I can't stop you. *You* have to stop *yourself* and then do some hard work to fix up your reading. If you think you're ready for that challenge, shout out, 'I can do this!'

"I can do this!" the students roared.

"Yes you can!" I reassured.

> ### Be a Reading Boss!
> If you think something's wrong, you've got to STOP!
>
> If you think something's wrong, you've got to STOP!
>
> If you think something's wrong, and you say, "What's going on?!"
>
> If you think something's wrong, you've got to STOP!

Readers Use *Everything* They Know to Solve a Word

IN THIS SESSION, you'll teach children that being in charge of their reading means using more than one strategy to figure out the hard parts, trying something and then something else to get the job done.

GETTING READY

✔ Post the new anchor chart for this bend, "Be the Boss of Your Reading!" in the meeting area, and prepare the next sticky note—"Try something ELSE to get the job done!" (see Connection).

✔ Display the "Good Habits for Solving Hard Words" chart from Unit 2 in the meeting area (see Teaching and Mid-Workshop Teaching).

✔ Return to your demonstration text for this bend, marking a page that spotlights a tricky word. We use page 4 of *The Dinosaur Chase*. You may decide to have students read a book from their book baggie during the active engagement (see Teaching).

✔ Set children up to bring their reading signs from Session 1 to the rug (see Teaching).

✔ Consider using the "Weekly Planning Sheet" to structure your conference time (see Conferring and Small-Group Work).

✔ Display the "Reading Partners Work Together" chart from Unit 2, and decide which of the routines students do with ease so you can remove the corresponding Post-it notes from the chart (see Transition to Partner Time).

✔ Write the second verse of "Be a Reading Boss!" on chart paper for children to sing (see Share).

MINILESSON

CONNECTION

Tell a short anecdote to highlight the idea that solving a problem means trying out more than one strategy.

"Readers, the other day I wanted to ride my bike—but I realized it was broken! So I called up my friend who has a job fixing bikes. I knew he would know what to do because he knows *everything* there is to know about bikes. So he looked at my bike and tried something—but it *still* didn't work! Do you think he just gave up?"

"No way!" called out a bunch of voices. I laughed.

"You're absolutely right. I was a little surprised because I thought he'd fix it fast. Instead, he stopped and looked everything over carefully." I tapped my finger on my temple with a thoughtful look on my face. "And then, he tried something *else*.

"Here is the important thing. My friend knew that if it was his job to fix the bike, he was going to have to think and try one thing. Then he'd have to think some more and try another thing. He knew he would have to try lots of different ways to fix the problem. I'm telling you this because you do the exact same thing when your reading breaks down. It's your job to take charge and do everything you can to fix it!"

❖ **Name the teaching point.**

"Today I want to teach you that if you are *really* in charge of your reading, you do everything it takes to figure out the hard parts. You try *something* and then try something *else* to get the job done!"

Add to the chart.

ANCHOR CHART

Be the Boss of Your Reading!

1. STOP at the first sign of trouble!
2. Try SOMETHING!
3. **Try something ELSE to get the job done!**

3. Try something ELSE to get the job done!

FIG. 2–1   Students eagerly hold up their hands to signal their teacher to stop—she's made a mistake in her reading.

TEACHING

Ask children to listen to you read and signal if you make a mistake. Then demonstrate how to use more than one strategy to solve the tricky word.

"Why don't we give that a try? I'm going to read the next part in *The Dinosaur Chase*, and it will be your job to spot any problems. Watch and listen carefully. If you ever notice that something's wrong, hold up your sign to signal '*Stop and try something.*'" I held up a reading sign to demonstrate.

"If you know the right word, don't call it out! Help me figure it out, but keep the word a secret." The kids nodded in agreement. I began to read from the beginning of the book, stopping after the first sentence on page 4:

> *Big Dinosaur went on walking (text says* waiting*)*
>
> *for a long, long, time.*

"Stop!" a bunch of kids shouted out, holding up their reading signs.

"Huh? Is there a problem?" I looked back at the book and reread to myself, "'Big Dinosaur went on walking.' Walking? That doesn't make sense. He's not walking anywhere," I exclaimed, pointing at the picture. Then, turning back to the kids, I said, "You're right. It looks like I have a job to do! Watch how I try something to fix it up. You tell me if it's all fixed up or if I need to keep on trying.

"Hmm, . . . what can I try?" I said looking puzzled. "I could look at the first part of the word. Let me try that." I placed my finger under the beginning of the word. "Walking!" I shook my head, looking confused. "The first part matches, but it still doesn't make sense. I'm going to have to try something *else*."

I looked up at the anchor chart, "Good Habits for Solving Hard Words." "I could look at the picture and think about what is happening. Let me try that. I see Big Dinosaur sitting outside the hole. He sure seems to be watching the hole

You'll want to be explicit in communicating and demonstrating that being a reader is all about being flexible, trying a variety of strategies, and persevering when faced with a problem. Make it clear that persevering is not what "good readers" do, excluding those who don't think of themselves as strong readers, but rather, is what all *readers do.*

In this demonstration you make an error typical of many readers at levels G and H. The miscue has many of the same letters as the word in the text, and while the error makes sense (a dinosaur could be walking), it doesn't make much sense in the context of the story. Here, you model the importance of always keeping in mind what's happening in the book to help monitor your reading.

carefully in case Little Dinosaur pops out. Maybe the word is *watching*. It starts with *w* and ends with *ing*. That could be the word."

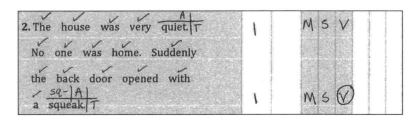

FIG. 2–2 You'll notice that this reader only makes one attempt or appeals for help before reading on. Your lesson today will be especially helpful for students like this.

> ### Good Habits for Solving Hard Words
>
> - Check the picture.
> - Look at ALL the parts of the word.
> - Get a running start.
> - Check it! Do a double-check!
> - Try it 2 ways!
> - Crash the parts together.
> - Do a <u>slow</u> check!
> - Say the word the best you can. Think about what it means.

ANCHOR CHART

I turned back to the class. "What do you think? Is it all fixed up, or do I need to keep trying? Thumbs up if you think I've got it." I scanned the class. "Uh-oh. Some of you don't agree. It looks like I haven't done my job yet. I have to try something *else*!"

"Let me look at *all* the parts of the word." I ran my finger under the word slowly saying, "W-ait-ing. Waiting! If I do a slow check, I can see that all the parts match *waiting and* it makes sense. Big Dinosaur is definitely waiting for Little Dinosaur to pop out." I stopped, running my arm across my forehead, as if wiping the sweat from my brow. "Phew! This word really made me work hard. Did I give up?"

"No!" the class boomed.

"No way! I put all those strategies together to figure out the hard part!"

ACTIVE ENGAGEMENT

Coach readers to try multiple strategies at the point of difficulty.

"Now it's your turn to get to work. Will you and your partner finish reading this page? Remember, if your reading breaks down, it's your job to take charge and fix it. Try something—and if that doesn't work, try something *else*. Ready, readers? Go!" Leaving the page under the document camera, I moved around the meeting area, listening in on partnerships reading.

Consider your students when planning this active engagement. If this text is too challenging for partnerships to read, have students read a book from their baggies as they did yesterday. However, don't worry if a few partnerships can read this text easily. Prompt these students to think about how they would help others with a word on the page. You might say, "Pick a word someone else might find tricky. What would you tell that person to try if he or she were stuck? What else could the person try?" Doing this thinking with known words still provides helpful practice that will transfer to harder texts.

"You can show your partner *how* to try out a strategy," I voiced over, in an attempt to get kids thinking a little more deeply about the problem-solving work. "Can you think of *something else* your partner can try to fix up the problem?" I then called the group back for a shared reading of the page.

LINK

Revisit the chart "Be the Boss of Your Reading!" to help students accumulate all that they've been taught. Invite children to read the chart along with you.

"Readers, you sure know what your job is when your reading breaks down. You know to stop and try *lots* of different things to figure out the word. You try something, and then something else, and then something *else*. Remember that when the books get harder, the words get harder. And when the words get harder, *your* job gets harder. So you need to . . ." I pointed to the first strategy on the chart, inviting the class to read aloud:

"'Stop at the first sign of trouble!'"

I continued, moving my finger to the next line of the chart and saying, "Then, you need to . . ."

"Try something!" the class called in response.

"But if that doesn't work," I said, "readers work *extra* hard and . . ."

"Try something *else* to get the job done!"

I responded, "That's right! Ready to try that starting right now? Off you go!"

As you listen to a few partnerships reading, gather some data about the strategies students cling to as word solvers. Do many children fixate on looking across the word, letter by letter? Are some only remembering to check the picture and think about the meaning of the story? Are others using nondescript language like "sound it out" to name their strategy? Keep this in mind as you plan for conferences and small groups that support readers to be more persistent and flexible word solvers.

FIG. 2–3 A chart written by a teacher, documenting the learning from each session

Moving Students toward Bigger Challenges

Identify the work that readers at particular levels are doing and encourage them to try new things.

As you confer with children, you may want to use this time to teach into the work that readers at various levels are doing, offering tips to address next steps. You might observe a child reading at level F, for example. You'll want to look for signs that he is searching for more visual information, looking across the word for known parts. Then you might say to the child, "I can tell that you're checking the *whole* word, saying each letter sound to figure it out. Now that you're reading longer words, reading one letter at a time can get pretty slow. So I want to remind you that not only can you look for letters you know, you can also look for whole parts you know to figure it out. Ready? Try it and I'll help you."

Similarly, you'll want to look for readers who have moved beyond level D but are still pointing, word by word. Coach these children to track the print with their eyes to improve fluency. You might quickly demonstrate how to reread the page by sweeping your finger under each line to wean children away from using their finger to read. Or you may provide readers with a simple tool, such as an index card or a clear plastic strip with the top edge outlined in a color to help students move line by line, rather than word by word. Be sure to monitor these readers closely, because you'll want to remove these scaffolds as soon as you can.

You might decide to quickly pull a small group of readers who are below benchmark to do some shared reading to stretch toward higher levels of text complexity. Choose an instructional-level text to read with the group, coaching students to read through unknown words, using all the parts of a word to decode. Depending on the length of the text, you might want to read it twice, allowing your voice to fall below your students' on the second read. Provide each child in the group a copy of the shared text to practice reading independently. Moving these readers toward benchmark levels will be critical, and you'll want to check in with them often, offering strategies to tackle the challenges at the next level of text complexity.

You won't want to neglect the needs of readers who are already reading above benchmark (level I or above). It's easy to devote the bulk of your time and energy to supporting the needs of your struggling readers, so you'll need to be strategic across your day and week to address the needs of every child, perhaps using a weekly planning sheet to structure your conference time. After all, it's just as important to help your highest readers continue to grow.

Use your time strategically, meeting with these children in partnerships. For example, you might introduce "twin books," giving copies of the same book to a pair of students, providing a book introduction and suggesting a strategy or two to help them tackle the challenges of the text. The level of the book you provide will depend on the work you want the students to practice.

MID-WORKSHOP TEACHING
Old Charts Can Help with *New* Work

"Readers, can I have your eyes up and over here for a moment?" I stood beside the "Good Habits for Solving Hard Words" chart and waited until all eyes were on me. "I've been listening to many of you, and you are not just remembering to *stop*. You're also remembering to *try something*. And I want to remind you of this tool in our room that can help you try something *else*. You can use the word-solving chart to think, 'What have I already tried? What *else* can I try?' Then, you can use *that* strategy to help you solve the word. Remember, readers use *everything* they know to solve tricky words. This chart can remind you of that."

"Readers, It's almost time for partner reading." I gestured toward the chart, "Reading Partners Work Together." "And I was just about to remind you to do these jobs today, but I'm thinking that there are things up here that you don't need a reminder for—things that are as easy as putting on your shoes! I'll bet that when you were little, putting on your shoes was a *big* job for you. You probably needed reminders and lots of help. But now, you get your shoes on your feet without hardly thinking about it. You don't need help! You just put them on your feet and go out the door!

"I'm thinking that there are some things on this partner chart that feel like putting on your shoes. You know exactly how to do them, you do them every day, and you don't need reminders! Take a look. Is there anything up here you do so well that we can take it off the chart?"

"We always sit side by side and put the book in the middle!" said Judy

"You're right! I never have to remind you to work as a team! That was a *big* job at the beginning of first grade, but not anymore! Let's take it off." We continued to read through the partner chart, identifying "We build good habits together," and "We read together" as other items that could be removed.

"Readers, you should be very proud of the way you have grown in your partner reading this year! Ready to make a stack of books and work together on these jobs with your partner? Off you go!"

ANCHOR CHART

Reading Partners Work Together

- We give reminders.
- We grow ideas together.
- We give book introductions.
- We don't just tell—we HELP!
- We do SOMETHING at the end.

Readers Try Something and Then Something *Else* to Fix Up Their Reading

Return to the class song to celebrate and encourage children to tackle trouble when reading.

"Readers, the hard work you did today deserves some celebration. Whenever your reading breaks down, the way my bike broke down, you need to take your job as a reader seriously and take charge. You need to try something and then try something *else* to fix it! You can't give up, or you'll just be stuck there.

"Let's sing together, starting with the first part of the song you learned yesterday, 'Be a Reading Boss.' Remember the tune? Sing with me!" I turned to the lyrics that I had written on chart paper:

Be a Reading Boss!

If you think something's wrong, you've got to STOP! *(clap, clap!)*

If you think something's wrong, you've got to STOP! *(clap, clap!)*

If you think something's wrong, and you say, "What's going on?!"

If you think something's wrong, you've got to STOP! *(clap, clap!)*

"Let's sing the next part to remember what you can do when your reading breaks down." I moved to the next verse on the chart:

Then you try something else, and don't give up!

Then you try something else, and don't give up!

Then you try and you try, and you say, "This job is mine!"

Then you try something else, and don't give up!

ANCHOR CHART

Be the Boss of
Your Reading!

1. STOP at the first sign of trouble!
2. Try SOMETHING!
3. Try something ELSE to get the job done!

16

Readers "Check It!"
to Self-Monitor

MINILESSON

IN THIS SESSION, you'll teach students that after solving a tricky word, readers always do a triple-check, asking, "Does that make sense?" "Does that look right?" "Does that sound right?"

CONNECTION

Compliment students on the work they have been doing so far in the unit.

"Readers, I noticed yesterday that you are getting really good at your new jobs. You've been remembering to stop and try *lots* of things when your reading breaks down. And I was thinking you are getting so good at those jobs that now you're ready for the next *big* job. What do you think? Are you ready for a *promotion*?"

"Yeah!" the group cheered.

Tell a brief anecdote to set children up for the teaching point.

"Do you remember the story I told you yesterday about my friend who fixed up my bike? Remember how he tried one thing, and when that didn't work he tried *another* thing before the bike was fixed?

"Well, after my friend fixed my bike I thought he was just going to give it back to me, but he didn't! Instead he said, 'Oh no, I have to check it first! What if I didn't fix it right?' So he hopped on the bike and tested the brakes and the wheels just to make super sure that the bike really was all fixed. Well, readers, just like my friend checked to be *absolutely* sure my bike was fixed, readers check to make sure they've got the right word. They do the 'triple-check'!"

GETTING READY

- Have the final Post-it for the "Be the Boss of Your Reading!" chart—"Check it! Do a triple-check!"—ready to add (see Connection).

- Choose a word in your demonstration text that you can use to model checking. We suggest *raced* on page 9 of *The Dinosaur Chase* (see Teaching).

- Choose two more words in your demonstration text that children can use to practice checking. Use Post-it notes to mask the words. Write a close but incorrect word on the first Post-it so students can check an incorrect attempt. We've chosen to write the word *beside* for *behind* on page 12. Write the correct word on the second Post-it so children can practice checking even when the word looks right (see Active Engagement).

- Write the third verse of the song, "Be a Reading Boss!" on chart paper for the children to sing (see Link).

- Set out colored pencils so students can add a check mark to their reading signs (see Mid-Workshop Teaching).

- Provide Post-it notes so students can mark challenging words (see Transition to Partner Time).

- Prepare a new chart titled "Tools for Solving and Checking Hard Words." Across the top write (or use Post-its), "Try Something!" and "Check It!" creating two columns. Then create three rows, writing, "Does it Make Sense?" "Does it Sound Right?" and "Does it Look Right?"—one in each row—in the right-hand column (see Share).

- Have the "Good Habits for Solving Hard Words Chart" from Unit 2 on hand. You'll be transferring some of the Post-its from this chart to the new chart, and others you'll drop entirely (see Share).

❖ Name the teaching point.

"Today I want to teach you that when you think you've read a tricky word correctly, you have to be the boss and check it. You can do a *triple*-check. Ask, 'Does it make sense? Does it look right? Does it sound right?'"

Add to the chart.

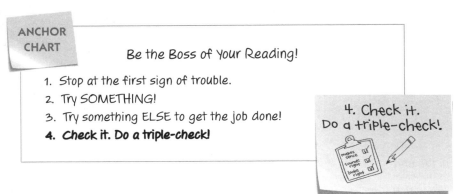

ANCHOR CHART

Be the Boss of Your Reading!

1. Stop at the first sign of trouble.
2. Try SOMETHING!
3. Try something ELSE to get the job done!
4. **Check it. Do a triple-check!**

4. Check it. Do a triple-check!

TEACHING

Emphasize the importance of doing a triple-check to make sure a word makes sense, sounds right, and looks right.

"Let's keep reading *The Dinosaur Chase*. Watch me carefully as I do some of this reading work right now. Watch to see if I stop when something is wrong and try something to fix it up. Then watch to see if I do a triple-check to make sure I read the word correctly before going on."

I reread page 4 of *The Dinosaur Chase* and quickly continued on to page 9, stopping at the word *raced*.

"'Little Dinosaur r–' What's this word?" I muttered to myself. I tapped the picture. "*Ran!* It must be *ran*, because I see him running! Guess I'm done." I brushed my hands together, looking back up.

"No! You have to triple-check!" a few voices called back.

"Oh right! Thanks, bosses!" I winked at the kids and pointed toward the chart. "Okay, let me check *all* three things to do a triple-check." I turned back to the book, held up a finger and said, "One. Does it make sense? 'Little Dinosaur ran away just in time.' Yup. That makes sense." I held up a second finger and said, "Two. Does it sound right?" I read the sentence again and nodded. "That sounds good."

I held up a third finger and said, "Three. Does it look right?" I put my finger under the first part and said, "Well, the *beginning* looks right." I slid my finger under the word. "Ra– Oh, no! The next part doesn't look right. I have to try

In this minilesson, you do two things. You further this bend's theme, that children have jobs to do, and you convey that they are ready to take on yet more work. Children will love the fact that they are getting a promotion and will be motivated to earn it.

When you teach children to ask themselves these self-monitoring questions, it is important that you coach readers to first ask, "Does it make sense?" You'll want your readers to understand that reading is first and foremost.

Be the Boss of Your Reading!

1. STOP at the first sign of trouble. STOP
2. TRY SOMETHING! tools
3. TRY something ELSE to get the job done!
4. Check it. Do a triple-check!

Using meaning, syntax, and visual information together helps readers to problem solve effectively. Explicit demonstration of this behavior may be necessary for some learners to understand what it means to "check" their attempts. This also helps students work with a greater sense of agency, not only doing something about a problem, but then taking the next step to check that work, all on their own.

something else!" I looked up at the word-solving chart. "Hmm, . . . Maybe I can try some of these letters two ways. I read the sentence again, this time trying out a few different sounds. "R-a-cked. No, that doesn't make sense. R-aced. Raced! 'Little Dinosaur raced away, just in time.' Yes, that makes sense, sounds right, *and* looks right. I triple-checked my reading to fix it up!"

ACTIVE ENGAGEMENT

Challenge children to help you solve two more tricky words in the demonstration text—one that you've read incorrectly and one that you've read the right way.

"Now it's your turn. I'm going to read on. There are some tricky words coming up. I already put what I *think* they say on Post-it notes, but I need you to help me check." I read on, stopping on page 12, where I had masked the word *behind* and written the word *beside* on the Post-it.

> Then Little Dinosaur
>
> raced down to the ferns
>
> that grew in the wet mud
>
> by the river.
>
> Big Dinosaur was
>
> right beside (behind) him.

I tapped the Post-it. "I think this word is *beside*. But you're in charge now, so can you check it? Turn and talk with your partner. Ask yourself, 'Does it make sense? Does it sound right? Remember to say why or why not. Then we'll come back together and check if it looks right."

I quickly listened in on a few partnerships before calling students back to check visual information.

"Great job checking, readers! I heard most of you say that *beside* sounds right, but some people weren't sure it made sense. It doesn't really look like Big Dinosaur is running *beside* Little Dinosaur. Something seems wrong. Let's *triple*-check. Check that *all* the parts of the word look right."

By writing the miscue on a label and masking the actual word, you give students an opportunity to check an attempt carefully. First, you'll prompt them to check that the word makes sense and sounds right. Then you'll reveal the actual word so that students can check whether your attempt looks right, too. If they do their job right, they'll see it doesn't match.

Then Little Dinosaur
raced down to the ferns
that grew in the wet mud
by the river.
Big Dinosaur was
right [beside] him.
Big Dinosaur was so big
that he made
the ground **shake**.

12

13

I peeled off the Post-it and placed it under the actual word in the text. "Does it look right? Is the word *beside*? Check all the parts of the word. Turn and talk." Again, I moved among the children, coaching partners with this work.

"Wow, readers, what great checking work you did. When you looked at *all* the parts of the word, you realized the word isn't *beside*. It's *behind*.

"Let's try one more word together." I continued down the page to where I had masked another word (*ground*), this time with the correct word on the label, giving students an opportunity to check a word that was read accurately.

LINK

Channel children to help you recap the steps readers follow when they encounter a tricky word.

"From now on, you have to be the *boss* of your reading, especially when words get tricky. I pointed at the first bullet of the chart. Number 1: First, you need to . . ."

"Stop!" the class chanted.

"Yes, then step 2: Try *something!* And if that doesn't work, step 3 . . ."

"Try something else to get the job done!" the kids filled in.

"And when you think you've got it, your job's not done: do the triple-check! That reminds me of the next verse of our song. Here it is. Sing it along with me!" I clipped the lyrics of the class song to the easel and pointed to the next verse:

> When you think you've got it right, check it out!
>
> When you think you've got it right, check it out!
>
> When you think you've got it right, triple-check with all your might . . .
>
> > Does it make sense?
> >
> > Does it sound right?
> >
> > Does it look right?
>
> When you think you've got it right, check it out!

After we sang, I transitioned the class to begin independent reading. "Ready to get to work? Off you go!"

Be sure to have children practice checking their reading, both when they have made an error and when they have solved the word correctly. Your readers will need to understand that after checking an attempt they either need to make another attempt or to verify that the word is correct before reading on.

If you use this book as your demonstration text, your students will no doubt be wondering how Little Dinosaur fares and takes charge to solve this very big problem! You will want to find another time in your day, perhaps during shared reading, to read through this text from beginning to end.

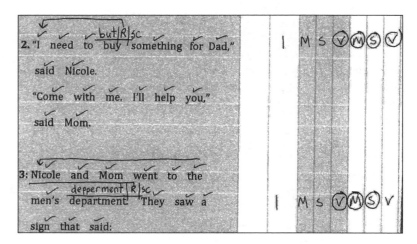

FIG. 3–1 After making an attempt, the reader went back and corrected the mistake, this time primarily using meaning and structure as additional sources of information. You'll want to see evidence of self-correcting from all your readers.

GRADE 1: READERS HAVE BIG JOBS TO DO

Analyzing Running Records to Inform Your Teaching

Use data from running records to decide what to teach.

Early on in this unit, you will want to use reading assessments, primarily running records, to analyze and develop whole-class goals for minilessons and shared reading, as well as to make brief plans for conferences and small-group instruction. For more information on taking and analyzing running records you'll want to refer to *A Guide to the Reading Workshop, Primary Grades*.

You will want to spend some time collecting updated running records on your kids. First, you'll want to determine both their independent (96% and above accuracy) reading level and their instructional (90–95% accuracy) reading level. Then you'll analyze the data by determining what sources of information (meaning, syntax, and visual) readers are using and not using. Look for patterns in a child's reading behavior to plan next steps.

For example, you might find groups of students who need to:

- Search for meaning, stopping to think about what's happening to determine a word that makes sense

- Monitor for syntax when their reading doesn't sound right

- Check all the parts of the word to use visual information more effectively, not just attend to the beginning of a word or decode letter by letter

(continues)

MID-WORKSHOP TEACHING
Using Tools as Reminders When Reading Breaks Down

"Readers, bosses use lots of tools to help them do their jobs well. I see many of you with your reading signs right next to you. When a word is tricky, your sign can remind you to stop, try lots of strategies and check it! Draw a big check mark on the 'Try Something' side of your reading sign!" I held mine up to show children what I expected. The children used colored pencils to draw a check mark on their signs. "Your reading sign is a great tool to help you. You can set it next to the book you're reading so you can remember what to do whenever your reading breaks down."

TRANSITION TO PARTNER TIME   Celebrating and Sharing a Tough Word You Solved with Your Partner

"Readers, I've noticed so many of you taking charge of your own reading." I moved to stand next to the chart. "In fact, when the words were tricky I noticed that you stopped, tried something, tried something else, and *then* checked that you got it right," I said, pointing at each strategy. It's time to celebrate all of this great work. Can you quickly find a word in your book where you took charge of your own reading? A spot where you tried something, then tried something *else*, and checked it? You might even find more than one spot. Mark it with a Post-it."

I gave children a moment to mark up their books. "Today, you might start your partner time by sharing the hard work you did to problem solve those tough words in your book. Don't just say what word you solved. Explain *how* you solved it. Then reread the books that you have stacked up! Okay, bosses, get to it!"

- Stop at the point of error to self-correct

- Develop more flexibility in the way they solve words, trying it one way and then another

Of course, you won't be able to meet with all children to help them do all of these things the first week; but you *can* strategically plan some small groups to teach into things like searching for meaning or checking the whole word across three or four days. You may pull students into some strategy lessons as they read their just-right books, or you could work with students in an instructional-level text. In any case, your analysis of running records will help you outline these plans.

Use the information you glean from assessments to decide how you will coach readers in conferences and small groups.

You might decide to start a small group of students who need to search for more visual information, using the *whole* word. Pull them together and say, "I want to remind you that readers don't just check the first part of a word and fill in something that starts the same way. They use the *whole* word and look carefully across *all* the parts to read." Coach readers to try it, giving lean prompts as needed, such as:

- Run your finger under this word and say it slowly.

- Say the first part. Say the next part. Say the last part.

- Does this part look like a part you know?

- Does the ending match?

- Check it! Do all the parts match?

Vary your methods to best target the needs of your readers.

As you work with children on these critical next steps, consider the *kind* of instruction that will most benefit your readers. You can pull children into one-on-one coaching conferences, or you can coach partnerships. You'll also form small groups of students who have common needs that you can address through strategy lessons, shared reading groups, and/or guided reading groups. You'll want to pull small groups together as quickly as possible and to work with them in efficient ways, helping them begin to identify and address clear, focused goals. (See *A Guide to the Reading Workshop, Primary Grades* for further information on these methods.)

Helping Readers Find the Right Tool for the Job

Revise the "Good Habits for Solving Hard Words" chart, creating a new chart entitled "Tools for Solving and Checking Hard Words" to help readers differentiate sources of information.

I hung the "Good Habits for Solving Hard Words" chart from previous units beside the meeting area as the children settled down. I pointed to the chart.

"This word-solving chart is full of so many tools to fix up tricky words that it might be hard to find the right one. Let's take the strategies we know and reorganize them on a new chart so they are easier to find. We could even pretend our chart is a tool shelf!" I clipped to the easel the chart that I had started, titled "Tools for Solving and Checking Hard Words." Across the top I had already written "Try Something!" and "Check It!" Under "Check It!" I had also written, "Does it make sense?" "Does it sound right?" and "Does it look right?"

Referencing the new chart, I began. "Readers, we already know that when a word gets tricky we need to try something," I said, my finger lingering on the chart, "and then . . ." "Check it!" the class filled in. "Right," I continued. You also know how to check that it makes sense, sounds right, and looks right. To help us stay organized, let's put all the strategies that help us check if a word makes sense together, just like we are storing them all on the same tool shelf! We could do the same for the strategies that help us check if it looks right and sounds right!"

FIG. 3–2   In this classroom, each child has a bin, or "library," where they keep their independent reading books and tools to support them in their reading.

I peeled off a Post-it from the original word-solving chart and read it aloud: "Check the picture."

"Hmm, . . . does this tool help us make sure the word makes sense, sounds right, or looks right? Well, checking the picture reminds us to think about a word that fits with what's happening in the story—a word that makes sense. So I'll put 'Check the picture' on this 'shelf' in the first column, right across from 'Does it make sense?' Now, where should this one go?"

I peeled off another strategy from the original chart, then read it aloud: "Look at *all* the parts of the word."

Hands raised in response. "Quick, turn and tell your partner which shelf this should go on, and be sure to explain *why*." I leaned in to assess students' responses.

"It should go on the shelf across from 'Does it look right?' because you have to look at the word," one partner explained.

After a brief moment, I called students back. "I heard some of you say this strategy helps us make sure the word *looks* right. Yes! When you check *all* the parts of the word, you can check that the word looks right and the letters match." I transferred the strategy to the new chart, and we continued moving the strategies from our original word-solving chart to the new-and-improved chart.

You can hand-write the names of the sections as shown, or use the Post-it notes supplied in the Anchor Chart Note pack.

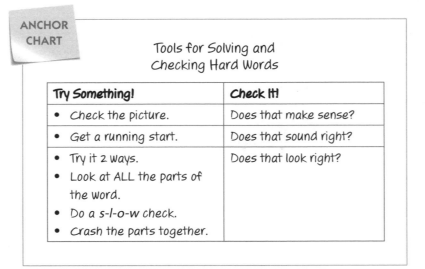

ANCHOR CHART

Tools for Solving and Checking Hard Words

Try Something!	Check It!
• Check the picture.	Does that make sense?
• Get a running start.	Does that sound right?
• Try it 2 ways.	Does that look right?
• Look at ALL the parts of the word.	
• Do a s-l-o-w check.	
• Crash the parts together.	

Readers Make a Plan

MINILESSON

In your connection, you might choose to compare today's work to the important self-assessment work your students do as writers. You might say, "During writing workshop, you don't just get to the end of your book and say, 'Done!' No way! You always reread your writing and use a checklist to remind yourselves of what you can do to make your writing even stronger. That way, *you* become stronger as a writer! But writers aren't the only ones who do that important thinking and planning. Readers do it, too."

Then, name the teaching point. Say, "Today I want to teach you that readers who are in charge have big plans for their reading. They think, 'What do I do *a lot*? What can I do even *more*?' and then they make a plan to be the best they can be."

In your teaching, you'll want to think aloud, studying the class word-solving chart like a checklist, naming what you know you do *every* time you get stuck on a tricky word. You might say, "Watch how I use the chart just like you use a writing checklist and think, 'What do I always do?' and 'What can I do *more*?' Well, I know that when I get stuck on a tricky word in my book, the first thing I *always* do is . . ." Then, reading each strategy aloud, you might pause to admit that there are one or two that you don't always use. "Hmm, . . . you know, I don't usually remember to . . . I think I should make a plan to do that *more*." You might decide to jot down this strategy on a Post-it as a reminder note for your independent reading time, making your plan more tangible.

During the active engagement, prompt readers to use the class chart as a checklist, perhaps giving each child a small copy of the "Tools for Solving and Checking Hard Words" (see online resources 👆) chart. Partners can work together to name the strategies they use all the time and those they don't use as often. Coach partners to circle the one strategy (or two) on their personal copy of the word-solving chart, making a plan for how they'll push themselves to use more strategies when they get stuck on a tricky word. Be sure to celebrate the reading plans students make, encouraging honest self-assessment and helping children establish a growth mind-set. Meanwhile, know that although you've been working on goal-setting in both reading and writing since the beginning of the year, some children will still have a "checklist" mentality; they'll check off every strategy on the list and announce that they do each and every one, all the time. Other kids might pick strategies that don't match what they need to prioritize. Don't worry about this. Right now it's enough to set children up to have goals and for you to assess the degree to which students are aware of their strengths and next steps. As you confer and meet with small groups, you'll help students adjust and hone their goals.

In your link, remind children to continue using the strategies they own while also pushing themselves to add more strategies to their tool belt. You might say, "When a construction worker gets a brand-new shiny tool, he doesn't throw out all the other tools on his belt. He uses *all* the tools to get the job done." You might invite the class to sing the "Be a Reading Boss!" song before sending students off to start their independent reading.

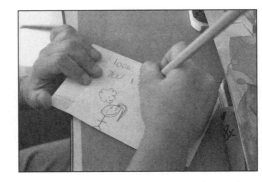

FIG. 4–1   Alyssa jots a new goal for herself as a reader.

CONFERRING AND SMALL-GROUP WORK

As you confer today, use the anchor chart as a checklist to form your own assessments of your students' use of reading strategies. What are kids doing with automaticity? Which skills will you need to revisit in the next bend? Use this time to set yourself up for future instruction. In addition, you might identify students who need help revising their goals, pulling them together in a quickly assembled small group to help them readjust.

Mid-Workshop Teaching

In your mid-workshop teaching, prompt readers to check in on their goals. Coach them to think, "Have I worked toward my goal? What can I do now to get stronger as a reader?" Remind them to keep their goals visible during reading workshop so they can stay focused on the strategies they're aiming to use more consistently. You might suggest that readers keep a running tally next to their goal(s) as a way to track how often they used the strategy during independent reading.

Transition to Partner Time

As you transition to partner time, suggest that children help one another check their goals. Have they chosen wisely? As one child reads, her partner might make a tally for each strategy used. Does the reading partner always look at the letters? Does she need to pay attention to whether the word makes sense? Reference your "Reading Partners Work Together" chart, explaining that checking in with each other about goals is another way to "give reminders."

SHARE

Today's share session offers students a chance to celebrate the goals they have chosen and to find a safe place to keep these. Children might affix the goal sheet to the front of their reading mat or book bag or perhaps find a "special spot" for the goals. Letting students take charge of where to keep their goals encourages them to keep these front and center in their minds. You could also set children up to share their goals with their families.

Readers Get Help When They Need It

MINILESSON

CONNECTION

IN THIS SESSION, you'll teach students that they can call on their partners to help them use strategies and check their reading, especially when it's really tough.

Explain that sometimes even bosses need help to solve problems.

"Readers, I'm so impressed with the way you've all been taking charge of your reading and fixing up the hard parts in your books. You're the kind of readers that don't back down from problems. You do something to solve them. But have any of you ever had a problem that really stumped you? You know, the kind of problem that made you try something and then something else, and something *else*, and something *else*, but you *still* couldn't figure it out?"

A few children nodded their heads in agreement. "I know it's happened to me before," I said, nodding.

"Guess what. Every single boss in the world faces problems like that—problems that are bigger than they can figure out on their own. It's true. It's happened to the principal. It's happened to the mayor. It's even happened to the president!" The children's eyes widened in disbelief. "It's true! And when that happens, they do one thing." I leaned in and cupped my hands around my mouth, dropping my voice to a whisper. "Here's the secret that only a boss is allowed to know. They ask for help—not just help to solve the problem, but help to get *better* at doing their job. And if you're the boss of your reading, you can too."

GETTING READY

✔ Display the "Tools for Solving and Checking Hard Words" and "Reading Partners Work Together" charts in the meeting area (see Connection).

✔ Prepare the new Post-it note—"We work together to solve hard problems."—for the partner chart (see Connection).

✔ Set one child up to join you in modeling the work of being a helpful reading partner (see Teaching and Active Engagement).

✔ Make sure to have a reading sign to use as you model (see Teaching and Active Engagement).

✔ Gather a piece of chart paper and markers to create a sign with your students for the classroom door (see Share).

✔ Add the final stanza of lyrics to the "Be a Reading Boss!" song that you've been writing on chart paper (see Share).

❀ **Name the teaching point.**

"Today I want to teach you that sometimes people need to *work together* to solve hard problems. You can call on your partner to help you use *lots* of strategies and check your reading, especially when it feels really tough."

Add to the chart.

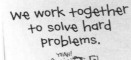

ANCHOR CHART

Reading Partners Work Together

- We give reminders.
- We grow ideas together.
- We give book introductions.
- We don't just tell—we HELP!
- We do SOMETHING at the end.
- **We work together to solve hard problems.**

We work together to solve hard problems.

YEAH!

TEACHING and ACTIVE ENGAGEMENT

Set students up to "fishbowl" a partnership, noticing how one partner helps the other with a challenging part of the text.

"Readers, I was thinking that today would be a good day for us to watch how reading partners can help each other when they run into *big* problems with their reading. Will you quickly make a circle around the meeting area, like a giant fishbowl? And Anthony, will you please join me in the middle of the fishbowl?"

I waited for the class to settle, and then I modeled reading the title, looking at the front cover, and taking a quick sneak peak at the first few pages. Then my partner and I decided to take turns reading.

While this lesson might seem somewhat contradictory to the message in the previous sessions (readers should solve problems independently), it's not. Giving children permission to seek out assistance from others helps them to take on even more ownership for their own learning. Think of a time you wanted to develop your expertise in an area—chances are you sought out the advice of a knowledgeable friend.

FIG. 5–1   Sitting in a fishbowl, the class watches carefully as Ms. Maddox and Ashley coach each other as readers.

You will want to take this opportunity to reinforce well-developed habits in partner reading. It is also important that children see our current focus on word solving as playing a supporting role to the bigger work of maintaining meaning. Don't miss this opportunity to show how partners should be thinking about their books before they read, maybe making a few predictions and settling in to enjoy the experience of sharing a great story with a friend.

I began reading and role-played getting stuck on a word and making a few quick attempts to solve it, using strategies from our "Tools for Solving and Checking Hard Words" chart. Anthony whispered and pointed to each step on our reading sign as I attempted to work through the word. Then I turned to Anthony and said, "Oh dear. This is a tough problem. Can we work on this together?"

"Sure!" Anthony responded enthusiastically.

I turned my attention back to the class. "Whoa. You actually saw us do a lot already. Can you quickly talk to your partners about *all* the things you saw so far?" As I listened, I repeated some of the ideas I wanted the group to notice. "Oooh. I heard someone say that we had great habits for our partner reading. We took a sneak peak and made a plan for our reading."

FIG. 5–2   Taking on the role of detectives, students turn their hands into notebooks and check off their observations.

Reconvene the group and restate the key observations students made.

"Readers," I said, bringing the class back together. "You did a great job of watching us work together. Let's take out our imaginary notebooks and check off what we saw." I reached into my pocket and turned my hand into a pretend notebook. "Somebody noticed that Anthony did not tell me the word when I got stuck. He let me work on the problem and waited for me to *ask* him for help with the word. Check that off if you noticed it as well." I put a check in my pretend notebook with a flourish. "Instead, he quietly helped me out by pointing to our reading sign, reminding me to try something and check it.

"And someone else noticed that even though the word was hard, I still tried my best to figure it out. I sure don't have that bad 'Tell me!' habit. I did ask Anthony to work on the problem with me, but only *after* I gave it my best try. Check that off if you noticed it!"

Give students a second chance to observe the partnership in action.

"Okay, keep watching to see how Anthony helps me now. Ready?"

I turned back to Anthony. "Let's work on this together. I could use a little help. What do you think I could do?" I gestured to a small version of our "Tools for Solving and Checking Hard Words" chart.

"I think you should go back and take a running start. That helps me think about what's going on."

"Okay," I said tentatively. "Um, . . . Anthony, can you remind me *how* to do that?"

"Just go back a little bit, maybe up to here," said Anthony, pointing to the beginning of the sentence, "and think about what's happening." I reread the sentence, articulated the first sound in the problem word, and this time, read the word accurately.

"I got it! It makes sense, looks right, and sounds right!" I said, modeling a very quick check of my word solving. I then continued reading the rest of the page before turning back to the class. "Readers, what did you notice about *how* Anthony helped me? Turn and talk."

I brought the group back together to highlight important observations. "Give your notebook a check if you noticed that Anthony *still* didn't tell me the word!" I said, peering down at my notebook and prompting the class to use one hand to represent their notes. A flurry of hands made a check sign. "Instead, he looked at our chart and thought about the best strategy I could try."

"He even showed you how to do it," added Parker.

"You're right! Good noticing. Partners don't just help us by giving us ideas, they can also remind us *how* to do those things. I hope you've learned some great tips for working with your partners today."

Notice how students are active participants in your teaching. By simply incorporating a little drama (checking off notes in an imaginary notebook), you'll keep children attentive and thinking alongside you. And of course, it's also extra fun!

LINK

Remind students that readers can call on partners to help them solve challenges in their books.

"Just like anybody who has an important job to do, you might find out that you run into big problems when you're reading. *After* you've tried your best to solve the problem, remember that you can call on your partner to help you—not to *tell* you the word, but to help you use *lots* of strategies and check your reading. This doesn't just help you solve your problem. It helps you do your job even better every day!"

FIG. 5–3 Ashley helps Javyn through difficult parts of a book by suggesting strategies to use and demonstrating them.

Coaching Partners to Use the Skills They've Learned

Coach partners to talk about what they read, supporting their ability to build conversation.

As you confer and work with small groups today, you may want to spend some time supporting partnerships in working together. First, take a little time to observe a partnership, seeing what they do independently.

It's important that partnerships don't jump from one book right to the next. Remind students to linger across the pages, pausing to comment before reading on, as well as at the end of the book. Guide students to turn to the class chart "Readers TALK About Books" (see Read-Aloud from Unit 1) to use these language stems to share ideas and questions. Remind partners to take turns talking and listening, responding to one another and building off of each other's points, both while they read and after. Help partners build conversation across multiple exchanges about the book.

Readers TALK about Books

"I think . . . because . . ."

"I wonder . . . Maybe . . ."

"I can add on . . ."

"Why do you think that?"

Listen to assess partner talk. Do partners say things like:

- This part is really . . . (funny, sad, surprising, and so on)

- I think . . . because . . .

- I wonder why . . . Maybe . . .

- What do you think?

- I also think . . .

You might say, "Joseph, when Marta said 'I think the boy's sister is really bossy,' you jumped to an idea about a different part of the story. Remember, it's your job to say 'I also think . . .' to keep the talk going. One thing you can do as partners is to make sure you both listen carefully to each other's ideas and push yourselves to add on to keep your talk going. So, Marta, when Joseph tells *you* an idea, you can try this, too. Let's try it together. Marta, start reading, then stop and share one idea you're having. Joseph and I will listen, and then we will try to *add* on and say, 'I also think . . .'"

Pull together a small group of a few partnerships that could use your guidance around a particular task.

Last, you may pull together two or three partnerships who you have noticed need similar help. Maybe you see that they tend to give their partners the word, rather than

---

MID-WORKSHOP TEACHING **Checking In on Goals**

"Readers, yesterday each one of you made some big plans for your reading. You thought of what you do a *lot* when you run into trouble and what you need to try to remember to do more. But remember, having a plan only helps if we do the things we plan to do! If you don't have your plan out, do that right now and think about how it's going. Are you remembering to make your reading stronger by practicing those strategies? If not, now's your chance to refocus and work toward your goals!"

"Today you got to watch me and a reading partner learn *how* to help each other through the tough parts in a book. Remember, working with a partner doesn't mean we fall back into that bad 'Tell me!' habit. It means we take charge and try our best before we ask for help to make our reading stronger. If you want to give your partner some help, you can suggest some ideas to try and then show him *how* to use those strategies. You might choose to switch books with one another. Partner 1 can read one of Partner 2's books first. That means Partner 2 will *help*, not just *tell* the word," I said pointing to the partner chart as a reminder of this strategy. "Instead, you can say, 'Remember to use your tools!' and then help your partner solve the word. Then, switch."

ANCHOR CHART

Reading Partners Work Together

- We give reminders.
- We grow ideas together.
- We give book introductions.
- We don't just tell—we HELP!
- We do SOMETHING at the end.
- **We work together to solve hard problems.**

We work together to solve hard problems.

YEAH!

teach them the strategies to use. Pull them quickly together and say, "I can tell that you are working hard to read words, even the tricky ones! But I want to remind you that when you read with a partner, and your partner is stuck, it's important to *help*, not *tell*. I have a new job for you. It's a job I do every day. That's right—help, just like a teacher! Use the charts in the room to give your partner a teacher tip. Say, 'You should try . . .' Then, help your partner *use* the strategy to figure out the word."

You might use a shared text to play the role of a partner who is stuck on a word. Coach students to suggest strategies without telling you the word outright. When you coach readers, focus on strengthening how they can work *better together* when reading with a partner.

Then, ask the students to turn to their partners and try working together again. Listen in to each partnership as they help each other, prompting them as needed. Make sure to name the positive things students are doing so that they will continue to be replicated in coming days. "You are paying careful attention to the book as your partner reads," you might say. "Your partner is lucky to have someone as thoughtful as you to work with. You didn't just jump in and tell her the word! You thought about the best tool that might help and made a great suggestion."

Celebrating Readers' Hard Work

Celebrate the learning of the first bend by singing the "Be a Reading Boss!" song, adding the final verse.

"Readers, you've been working so hard doing important reading jobs." I held up a finger to count out each job as I recapped students' work across the week. "You know that whenever you notice trouble, you stop, try something, and keep on trying! When you've fixed up the problem, you do a quick check to make sure you've got it right. You've even made a plan and learned how to work with a partner to get better as a reader.

"Already, in just a few days, *you* have learned how to be the boss of your reading! Let's sing the 'Be a Reading Boss!' song again and add one more verse to celebrate! It goes like this":

> Be the boss of your reading, be the boss!
>
> Be the boss of your reading, be the boss!
>
> When the job gets really tough,
>
> And you want to huff and puff *(cross arms and sigh)*
>
> Be the boss of your reading, be the boss!

"Let's sing it from the top and let the whole school know the big *jobs* readers do!" With a proud smile, I pointed to the lyrics on the chart paper as we sang through the song from beginning to end.

"I think the whole school definitely heard that!" I laughed. "Wait a minute," I said thoughtfully as if just getting a brilliant idea. "I bet they're all wondering what this celebration is about. I think *everybody* needs to hear about the work you've been doing. Let's make a sign to tell them!"

"Yeah!" shouted the class.

Use interactive writing to make a sign for the classroom door as a way to create a buzz in the school about the important reading work students are doing.

Grabbing a piece of poster paper and a marker I quickly wrote "CAUTION!" on the top. "It could be just like the signs we see on the road when people are hard at work doing their job, only our sign could say, 'Caution! *Readers* at Work!' Can you help me out? First, we need to write the word *readers*. Let's all say it slowly and think about what sounds we hear." I called up one child, then another, to record parts of the words to make the sign, as the rest of the class practiced spelling the words by tracing the letters in the air. We quickly finished the sign, and with great fanfare, posted it on the outside of our classroom door.

"There! Now everyone will know about all the hard work going on in here. High fives all around for a job well done!"

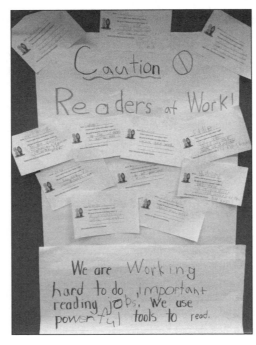

FIG. 5–4 Each child posted a reading goal on this chart. The class then added a message to share with the school community.

Readers Add New Tools to Read Hard Words   BEND II

Readers Think about the Story to Problem Solve Words

IN THIS SESSION, you'll teach students to think about what is happening in the story to help them problem solve a difficult word.

GETTING READY

✔ Have the strategy Post-it note—"Think about what's happening."—ready to add to the "Tools for Solving and Checking Hard Words" chart (see Connection). 👆

✔ Choose a new demonstration text a little above benchmark level to use throughout the bend. We use *Zelda and Ivy: The Runaways* (level J), but the teaching points in this bend will transfer to whatever text you choose (see Teaching and Active Engagement).

✔ Use Post-its to mask several words in your demonstration text so you can model, and children can practice, word solving. Leave the first letter or two visible. We suggest the words *miss* and *cucumber* on page 5, and *hungry* on page 6 in *Zelda and Ivy*. If you choose your own mentor text, be sure to select words that can be solved by thinking about the story (see Teaching and Active Engagement).

✔ Display the "Partners Work Together" chart and prepare the new Post-it note—"We keep track of what's happening." (see Transition to Partner Time and Share). 👆

MINILESSON

CONNECTION

Celebrate students' growth, and invite reading partners to give each other compliments.

"Readers, I'm sure you've seen the great reading work your partners have been doing because you read with them every day. In fact, I bet you could give them a compliment! Instead of just saying something like 'good job,' be specific. Say, 'I notice you always check tricky words,' or 'Wow, you stop right away if something's wrong!' Right now, quickly turn to your partners and compliment them on something they do when reading gets tough." The room erupted into a flurry of compliments for a moment before I brought the class back together.

Explain that readers sometimes use bigger tools to get the job done.

"Hearing all these compliments has sure got me thinking. Now that you're so great at all of these jobs, you must be ready for some even bigger challenges. But here's the thing about big jobs: the tougher the job, the bigger the tool you need. If somebody is building a house, for example, that person would have little jobs and big jobs to do. For a little job, like putting in a mailbox, the person could just grab a shovel off the shelf. But a bigger job would need a *bigger* tool—something more powerful, like a bulldozer! Are you ready to use some bigger, more powerful tools in your reading?"

"Yeah!" the class shouted back.

"Oh, I knew you'd be up for the job!" I smiled. "Well," I said, pointing at the word-solving chart, "Let's start here with this tool, 'Check the picture.' We need to make this tool as big as a bulldozer!"

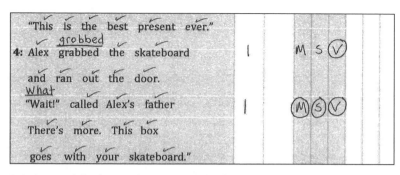

"This is the best present ever."

4: Alex grabbed the skateboard
grobbed

and ran out the door.

"Wait!" called Alex's father
What

There's more. This box

goes with your skateboard."

| I | M S Ⓥ |
| I | Ⓜ Ⓢ Ⓥ |

FIG. 6–1   While this reader uses visual information to try solving words, she is not yet using meaning consistently. Readers with a pattern of making miscues like this will especially benefit from today's session.

In the first unit, Building Good Reading Habits, *you taught children to look at the picture to search for meaning. As books become more complex, the pictures become less supportive and in some cases can actually be misleading. This session teaches students not just to think about what is happening on one page, but also to hold on to previous parts of the text, in essence summarizing to help them use meaning as a source of information.*

✤ Name the teaching point.

"Today I want to teach you that readers don't just look at the picture. They also think about what is happening in the story to help them figure out what word would make sense."

Add to the chart.

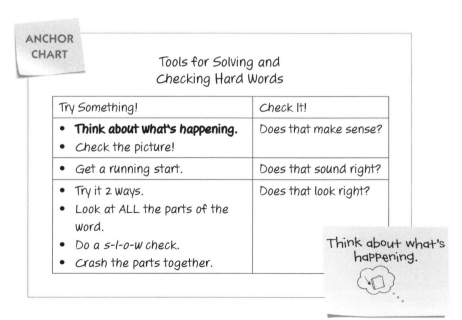

ANCHOR CHART

Tools for Solving and Checking Hard Words

Try Something!	Check It!
• **Think about what's happening.** • Check the picture!	Does that make sense?
• Get a running start.	Does that sound right?
• Try it 2 ways. • Look at ALL the parts of the word. • Do a s-l-o-w check. • Crash the parts together.	Does that look right?

Think about what's happening.

Tools for Solving and Checking Hard Words

Try Something!		Check It!
Think about what's happening.	Check the Picture.	Does that make SENSE?
Get a running start.		Does that SOUND right?
Try it 2 ways.	Look at ALL the parts of the word.	Does that LOOK right?
Do a s-l-o-w check!	Crash the parts together.	

TEACHING

Demonstrate how checking the picture is not always enough. Then, think about what has happened so far to determine a word that makes sense.

"Let me show you what this new tool looks like, so you'll be able to use it in your own books. Just yesterday I found this great book, *Zelda and Ivy: The Runaways*, in our classroom library. I'll read a little bit of it, and if I get stuck, will you remind me to think about the big things that are happening in the story?"

I read the title of the chapter and continued reading straight through the first few pages, stopping at the masked word (*miss*) on p. 5.

"Looks like I've got some work to do here! Well, I can see from the picture that Mom and Dad are in the house. But that doesn't help me figure this out," I said tapping the masked word. "Let me try again. I think I need a better tool to help me with this job." I glanced back at the chart. "Let's try thinking about what's happening in the story." I left a little silence for children to think alongside me.

I held out one finger, "Zelda and Ivy's dad made cucumber sandwiches for lunch," and then another finger. "And Zelda and Ivy didn't want to eat the sandwiches so they ran away. And now they think their mom and dad will . . . Wait! Could this word be *miss*, because now that they're gone, maybe their parents will *miss* them? That makes sense!" I peeled away the Post-it and reread the sentence to quickly check the letters. "It looks right, too! Readers, did you see how I did that? When the word was tough, I quickly thought to myself, 'What is happening in the story?' and that helped me think of a word that made sense."

In this lesson you'll read through a few pages of the book so that when you model a quick summary of the text, students will be able to do it right along with you. To keep your pacing tight, don't linger in these early pages, because you'll want to make sure your teaching point stands out.

ACTIVE ENGAGEMENT

Invite children to read the next page along with you. Then, remind readers to think about what is happening in the story to figure out a "hard" word in the text.

"Readers, now it's your turn to try this new tool. Let's read on a little bit, and when we come across another tricky word, will you remember to stop and think, 'What's happening on this page? What else has happened in the story so far? What word would make sense here?'" The children nodded. I read on, inviting students to chime in with me:

> *"Mom and Dad will really miss us,"*
>
> *said Ivy.*
>
> *"Yes," said Zelda "They'll be sorry they*
>
> *made us c_ _ _"*

The fox sisters peeked through the bush at their parents.

"Mom and Dad will really miss us," said Ivy.

"Yes," said Zelda. "They'll be sorry they made us cucumber sandwiches."

5

To allow for successful practice of this strategy, it will be critical that you think carefully about which words to mask. Ask yourself if you could solve the word by thinking about the meaning of the story. Leaving the first letter uncovered will also give kids the opportunity to use some visual information.

I halted abruptly. "Uh-oh, readers, looks like it's time to put your new tool to work. Will you *just* check the picture?"

"No!" the class answered.

"You're right. Remember to also think about what is happening on this page and what has happened in the story so far." I gave partners a moment to recap. "Okay now, readers, think, 'What could this word be? What word would make sense here?' Turn and talk." I moved in to listen as children deliberated.

Highlight the work of one partnership to reinforce the new strategy.

"Readers," I said, pausing for the class's attention. "I saw so many of you hard at work! Ethan and Vicki realized that the picture doesn't help much here. All you see is Zelda and Ivy peeking out from behind the bush. Then I heard Ethan and Vicki retell what's happened in the story so far and think, 'What could this word be?' Well, they said that first Dad made Zelda and Ivy cucumber sandwiches, and then they ran away. Vicki thought, maybe that's what Zelda is saying, "They'll be sorry they made us c-cucumber sandwiches!" Yes, that makes sense. Thumbs up if you and your partner agree too!" The children gave a thumbs up. I peeled away the Post-it to confirm.

"Let's try another one!" I reread the page before stopping at the word *hungry* on page 6 to give students one more opportunity to practice the strategy. Then I brought the class back together.

LINK

Recap the strategy to add this new tool to students' repertoire of word-solving strategies.

"Okay, readers, now you have a new tool to help you with your reading work! Add it to your tool belt. Wait! Our tools are getting much too *big* for a tool belt. Put it in your big toolbox! I bet you'll need it to fix up your reading today—and anytime you read!" I acted as though I was lifting a heavy tool to put it in an enormous (albeit imaginary) toolbox. "Whenever you get stuck on a tough word, it's not enough to just look at the pictures. Make sure you *also* ask, 'What's happening in the story?' to help you think of a word that makes sense."

While we know readers always use meaning, syntax, and visual information together when problem solving, we are angling this in a way that puts an emphasis on meaning. Don't worry! Your students will have ample opportunity to integrate other sources of information in the coming sessions.

"I'm a little hungry," said Ivy.

"We can't give in," said Zelda, "or we'll be eating cucumber sandwiches for the rest of our lives."

6

Using Guided Reading to Move Kids to New Levels

Identify students who seem ready for texts at the next level up.

As you start this next bend, you will want to be thinking about students who are ready to move into a new level of text and use guided reading as a method to support these students. You will want to pay particular attention to students reading below expectations for this time in the year. These children will benefit from meeting with you more frequently to accelerate their progress.

Select the text carefully, keeping your students in mind.

Make sure you carefully consider the instructional-level text you choose to use with your guided reading group. Think about whether it is a book this group would find interesting and be motivated to read. Then think about how much problem solving kids will have to do to read the text. Are there many difficult words, unusual language structures, or misleading pictures? Do children have enough background knowledge to

understand the context of the book? You'll want kids to have a few opportunities for problem solving, but these should be problems that students have the tools to solve.

Give a book introduction that supports a successful first reading of the text.

Start your guided reading group with a book introduction that sets your readers up for success. Taking the time to select the right text will pay off here, because you will have already anticipated the trouble that kids will run into. Now use your book introduction to prepare your readers for these challenges.

Be sure to include some of the same words and language structures that are in the book. This way, when the child who knows very little about sled dogs gets to a page with the word *husky*, she will have already heard the word in your book introduction and will be able to draw from this knowledge. You may also want to use some of the language structures from the book (for example, "where oh where . . ." or "down came the . . ."), exposing kids to the way the book "talks" prior to reading it.

Be sure not to show students *all* the hard parts in the book. Leave a few places where they have to productively struggle and use all they know to solve problems. You'll also want to make sure not to give away the whole book. You might finish your introduction by saying, "Let's read to find out . . . ," giving your readers an authentic purpose to finish the text.

Coach students through their initial reading of the text with quick prompts on the run.

As students read, you'll want to move from child to child, using lean prompts to coach into their problem solving. Try to use much of the same language you have on your charts to help students internalize the prompts. You'll need to listen carefully and get good at deciding what prompts will be the most helpful to a reader on the run, tapping into sources of information the child is not yet using. For example, if the child read, "He got a gold medal," when the text says "He got a golden medal," you will *not* want

MID-WORKSHOP TEACHING
Readers Reread to Remember What's Happening

"I've noticed that lots of you are remembering to ask yourselves, 'What is happening in the story?' as you stop and try to solve a tricky word. But I also noticed that a few of you ran into trouble when you tried this out. You started to think about the story and then said, 'Oops! I don't really know what's going on!' Readers, that's a problem that can happen to every single one of us. And here's a tip for when that happens. Ready?" I paused to make sure I had everyone's undivided attention.

"As soon as you realize that you don't know what's happening in your book, flip back to the part you *do* remember. Then, *reread*. Start reading again from that spot! But this time pay careful attention to what's going on!"

"Reading partners don't just help each other fix up tricky words. They also help each other keep track of what's happening in a book." I added, "We keep track of what's happening." to our partner chart.

ANCHOR CHART

Reading Partners Work Together

- We give reminders.
- We grow ideas together.
- We give book introductions.
- We don't just tell—we HELP!
- We do SOMETHING at the end.
- We work together to solve hard problems.
- **We keep track of what's happening.**

we keep track of what's happening.

☆ This Just In...

"I want to teach you how to play a game called 'This Just In!' When reporters have important news that they want their audience to know right away, they say, 'This just in,' and then they report the news. To play the game, you'll each pretend to be a reporter who has news to tell about your book.

"I'm going to give you four special Post-it notes. Before you start reading with your partner, decide which book you are going to read first, and put these Post-its in that book. You'll need to spread your Post-its across the beginning, middle, and end of the book." I quickly modeled how to flag pages.

"Start reading, and when you get to a page that has a Post-it on it, decide who will play the news reporter first. The reporter then holds up the microphone and says, 'This just in!' and tells what just happened in the book.

"Let's pretend that I'm Eliza's reading partner." I gripped my hand around an imaginary microphone, touched my ear piece with my other hand, and said, in my most dramatic voice, "We're interrupting this story to give you an important update. This just in: The big bad wolf has just blown down *another* house. That's right, he huffed and he puffed and he *blew* the straw house down. Partner 1, back to you!

"Readers, remember that when you're all finished reading one book, you can move your Post-its to another one and play again! Ready? Get started right now!" I moved quickly around the room, handing out special colored Post-it notes for each partnership to use.

to prompt with the question, "Does that make sense?" The child's version *does* make sense. Instead you might prompt, "Check it! Look across the whole word," directing the reader to use more visual information to fix this error efficiently. Pay careful attention to problems that seem to be common to the group, because you will address these after reading.

Check in on comprehension and provide a teaching point to move students forward.

You might have a short conversation after reading, perhaps having students retell and discuss the story to check for comprehension, and then supply a teaching point based on your observations. For example, if you noticed that several students were very focused on decoding words but were losing meaning, you might teach them that

readers *always* keep track of what's going on as they read. You could model how to stop after a page or two of the text to remind yourself of what is happening, predict what might happen next, and then read on. Coach students to practice this strategy with a few pages of their own copies of the text.

You'll want to finish your group in no more than ten minutes. If you have some time left, you could have students reread the text a second time.

Once you know students can read the book successfully, it is critical that children add the book to their book baggies after your guided reading lesson. In this way, you'll be giving kids access to instructional-level books, gently stretching them into a new level. After a second or third read, these books should be easy for the children to read independently (with 96–100% accuracy).

Partners Retell the Big Events

Remind children that readers do *something* at the end. Channel partners to retell the big events of the story, to act as reporters giving a full news report about their books.

"Will you come to the meeting area with your baggie and sit beside your partner?" Children gathered quickly and I began. "Thumbs up if you and your partner played 'This Just In' to read together." The children held their thumbs up high. "Double thumbs up if that game helped you keep track of the story." The children held up both thumbs.

"Well, don't forget that reading partners do *something* at the end of a book, too. You can retell!" I gestured toward the bullet on the partner chart that said, "We do SOMETHING at the end." "Instead of a short news update about the book, you can give a full news report, retelling *all* of the important parts. Like this." I folded my hands in my lap as if delivering the evening news. "I'm here to tell you about the story of Goldilocks and the Three Bears. It all began when Goldilocks smelled porridge while walking through the woods."

I shifted back to address the class. "Start at the beginning and retell the big events in order. And if you can't remember some of the details, your partner can help you add on. Ready to report on the books you read today? Okay, reporters, take out one of the books that you and your partner read. Then, give a full news report. Retell the big events to explain what happened at the beginning, in the middle, and at the end." I leaned in to coach partners to retell sequentially and name the big events of the story. I prompted children to help their partner fill in details, when needed, or to reread to remember more.

FIG. 6–2 Reporting on all the events of a great book

Session 7

Readers Think about What Kind of Word Would Fit

MINILESSON

IN THIS SESSION, you'll teach students that readers listen carefully as they read to consider what word might come next, thinking, "What kind of word would fit here?"

CONNECTION

Make up a short oral story to help students understand how their knowledge of language structures can help them predict words in a sentence.

"I have a friend who has this habit of finishing my ideas for me. She'll jump in and say the words before I can even get them out of my mouth! Has that ever happened to you?" A few heads nodded in agreement.

"Well, today I thought you could try to be like my friend. I'm going make up a little story. You listen carefully and think about what the next word might be. When I stop, I'll point to someone to say the next word. Let's try it!

"It was a beautiful hot sunny day, and so I decided to go to the . . ." I looked expectantly into the group, giving them a few seconds to think, and pointed to Sean. "Beach!" he shouted.

I took Sean's suggestion and continued on with my story. "'I love the beach,' I said to myself as I grabbed my bag and started to pack all the things I would need. I got out my swimsuit, my sunscreen and my . . ." I pointed to Judy. "Towel," she added.

"I couldn't wait to get to the beach, jump in the water, and start . . ."

"Surfing!" grinned Anil.

GETTING READY

✔ In your demonstration text, mask a few words that children can solve using syntax, leaving the first letter in each word visible. We suggest *cards* on page 7, *tonight* on page 8, and *talking* on page 11 of *Zelda and Ivy*. If you choose your own demonstration text, be sure the words you select can be solved by using syntax (see Teaching and Active Engagement).

✔ Prepare the strategy Post-it note—"Think what kind of word would fit."—to add to the "Tools for Solving and Checking Hard Words" chart (see Link and Mid-Workshop Teaching).

✔ Have student writing folders accessible for revising (see Share).

"Let's pause our story for a bit." I said with a laugh. "Did you notice how every time I stopped for a word, you had an idea for me? Like when I said 'I decided to go to the . . .' you were all thinking of *places* that I could go. You knew that word had to be a place. It was the only kind of word that would *sound* right! And when I said 'I couldn't wait to jump in the water and start . . .' you were all thinking of things I could do—*action* words like *swimming* or *splashing* or *surfing*! That's the kind of word that sounds right in *that* spot.

"You sure know a lot about how words and sentences work. When you listened carefully to what I was saying, you knew that certain words sounded right in certain spots. That helped you think of the next words in my story! Readers can do the same thing to work on tricky words in their books."

❖ **Name the teaching point.**

"Today I want to teach you *another* tool readers use to get their job done. They listen carefully as they read to consider what word might come next. They think 'What would sound right? What kind of word would fit here?'"

TEACHING

Demonstrate how to solve an unknown word by stopping and thinking about the *kind* of word that would sound right.

"Watch how I use this new tool to help me read on in *Zelda and Ivy*." I opened up to page 6 and began rereading the text to remind students of where we left off. I stopped at the Post-it on page 7, covering all but the first letter of the word *cards*.

> *"Lucky you brought your c_ _ _ _"*

"Oh! I'm stuck. But wait, I've got a *new* tool to try. Let me reread and think, 'What would sound right? What kind of word would fit here?' I see Ivy peeking in the window," I said tapping the picture. "Lucky you brought your peeking?" The class giggled. "*That* doesn't sound right! It's definitely *not* the kind of word we need here! I better try again."

I reread the line. "Well, it sounds like they brought *something*, so this word must be a thing. Hmm, . . . Lucky you brought your . . . teapot? That sounds right. Oh, but it has to start with a *c*. Let me try again. What's something they brought that starts with a *c*?" I waited a moment to give students an opportunity to think along with me. "Thumbs up if you're thinking it might say, 'Lucky you brought your cards.' Or, 'Lucky you brought your cups.' Those both sound right and they make sense. Let's take a look at all the letters and see if we can get some more clues.

I slowly peeled off the Post-it, revealing the whole word, and ran my finger under the word as I read it. "'Lucky you brought your cards!'

Children are bound to offer a variety of possibilities, and the aim is not to guess the exact word you had in mind, but instead to celebrate suggestions that fit the syntax (and meaning) of the sentence. For example, if a child says "pool" instead of "beach," follow their lead.

You won't want this work to be teaching the parts of speech or defining these for children. Instead, help children use the structure of English to anticipate what kind of word comes next in a sentence. For example, if you—a proficient reader—were to read, "Then, the dog . . ." you might anticipate that the next word could be ran *or* barked. *You'd use what you know about how the English language works to anticipate a verb. This lesson is intended to help children use what they know about oral language, not to learn parts of speech.*

Some students may not understand what it means to make their reading "sounds right." Here, you use a non-example (using a verb in place of a noun) to help make this idea clear. It definitely doesn't sound right! Using a non-example can be a powerful teaching tool to help students understand new concepts.

"Did you see how I was thinking about the kind of word that would sound right in the sentence? This helped me find a word that would fit. Then I checked to see if it looked right!"

ACTIVE ENGAGEMENT

Continue reading, but this time ask students for help in anticipating the next word, thinking, "What kind of word would sound right?"

"I'm going to keep on reading. This time, listen carefully, and when I stop, think about what word might come next. Just like you did with my story. Then, just shout it out! There might be some words we all know, and then we can keep on reading. But there might be other words that we have to really slow down and figure out. Ready? Let's read!"

I reread page 7 quickly before continuing on to page 8:

> "Be tough," said Zelda. "We may have to sleep here to_ _ _ _ _."

I paused at the masked word (*tonight*) and looked expectantly at the students.

"Tonight!" the class shouted.

I quickly peeled off the Post-it, revealing the rest of the word, and continued on to page 11 before stopping again. I read:

> When they finished, they could hear
>
> their parents t_ _ _ _ _ _

"They could hear their parents t_ _ _ _ _ _." I paused. "Hmm, . . . Let's stop to think about this one. I'll read the sentence again, and then you can turn and talk. What kind of word would sound right here? What word would fit?" I reread the sentence and gave partners a brief chance to talk. While they worked, I voiced over a few suggestions.

"I heard someone say the parents are doing something here, so this word must be an action! Did you notice that it starts with a *t*?"

"Let's take a look" I said, pulling the class back together. "I heard somebody say that the word might be *telling* or *talking* or *teasing* or *taking*. Those are all action words that would sound right!" I reread the sentence. "When they finished, they could hear their parents . . ." and peeled off the Post-it to reveal the word *talking*. "'When they finished, they could hear their parents talking and laughing in the kitchen.' That sounds right, makes sense, and looks right!"

Be sure to leave the first letter or two visible on each masked word. It's important that kids still have some visual information to help them predict the next word. This way, they'll understand that reading is not about making guesses. In this case we have limited the visual information kids are able to use to encourage them to think about the language structures.

You'll want to read a reasonable amount of text before stopping again to problem solve in order to help children get a sense of both the story and the language structures of the text. You also don't want to inadvertently send the message that reading involves a great deal of stopping and getting stuck. Your reading should be, for the most part, well phrased, fluent, and meaningful.

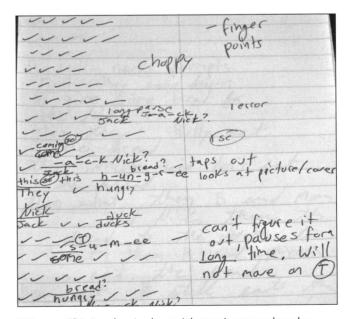

FIG. 7–1 This teacher took a quick running record as she listened to a child read his independent book. The teacher recorded the reading, made some quick notes about the behaviors she saw, and will return to this later to analyze the miscues and make a plan for further instruction.

LINK

Review students' growing repertoire of strategies, rereading the word-solving chart before adding today's new tool.

"Readers, your toolbox is filling up with tools. You've got tools that you've been using for a long time and tools that you're just starting to use. Let's reread our word-solving chart to quickly remind ourselves of all the things we can try to do when our job as readers gets tough." We read through the "Tools for Solving and Checking Hard Words" chart together.

"And don't forget, now you've got one more *new* tool to try! Remember, you can listen carefully to your reading, and when you get to a tricky word you can think about the kind of word that might come next. Ready to read now? Off you go!"

Add to the chart.

ANCHOR CHART

Tools for Solving and Checking Hard Words

Try Something!	Check It!
• Think about what's happening. • Check the picture!	Does that make sense?
• **Think what kind of word would fit.** • Get a running start.	Does that sound right?
• Try it 2 ways. • Look at ALL the parts of the word. • Do a s-l-o-w check. • Crash the parts together.	Does that look right?

Think what kind of word would fit.

park   jump   tiny

Learning from Running Records

Use running records on an ongoing basis to monitor student growth and reflect on your teaching.

Considering that this bend focuses on helping students solve words independently, you'll want to continue gathering all the information you can about the ways your students are tackling challenges when reading. Think of quick running records as a tool you can use to monitor your students' progress throughout the entire unit. These don't have to be formal assessments. Simply pull a chair next to a child as she reads a text from her book bag or a new text you've selected from the classroom library, and then record the reading on a blank sheet of paper. You'll want to keep in mind that

if the child is reading a familiar book, there will be fewer challenges for you to study. Also, don't feel like you need to listen to the child read the whole text. Just a few pages (ideally 100–150 words) will be sufficient.

Study these records carefully. Look for evidence of your teaching in the work you see the child doing. You may notice that the child who had the tendency to stop and get stuck is now making multiple attempts to solve a word independently. You'll want to compliment your students on these gains even if they seem tentative. A little positive affirmation from you will encourage children to repeat the behaviors, getting stronger each time.

(continues)

MID-WORKSHOP TEACHING
Readers Think about How Books Talk

"Readers, can I stop you for a minute? I see so many of you listening to yourselves as you read and thinking, 'What would sound right?' I wanted to let you in on a little secret. Did you know that books sometimes talk a little differently from the way we talk in real life? For example, a book might say 'Once upon . . .'" I trailed off, inviting kids to fill in.

"A time!" the group shouted.

"Exactly. If I was talking to my friends I wouldn't say, 'Once upon a time,' but a book might. You also know that after somebody is talking in a book, the next word is usually something like 'said,' or 'shouted,' or 'cried.' You probably won't hear Michael say 'Let's go to the gym, *said* Michael.' But *books* talk this way! Remember, readers, you know a lot about the special ways that books talk. You can keep this in mind to help you think about what might come next!"

TRANSITION TO PARTNER TIME
Checking that the Reading Sounds Right

"Readers, will you put a thumb up if you've been listening carefully to yourself while you read?" Children indicated that they had. "Listening to your reading can help you think of the word that might come next, but that's not all! Listening while you read also helps you notice when something is wrong. Like if I was reading and said, 'I *wented* to the park,' I'd probably realize, 'That doesn't sound right!'

"Well the great thing about reading with a partner is that now there are *two* sets of ears to listen carefully. Whoa! That's *four* ears to do this careful listening and checking work. As you are reading together today, can you listen *extra* carefully to not just your own reading, but also to your partner's reading?" I said, cupping my hand around my ear and looking intently. "As soon as something doesn't sound right, you can say 'Check it! That doesn't sound right!' and then help your partner fix it up. Get to it!"

You may also find cases in which students do not demonstrate changes in their reading. When this happens, reflect on your teaching. Was it simple and clear? Did you demonstrate the strategy you want children to use? Did they have many opportunities to practice the strategy with your support? Remember that you can give the most beautiful demonstrations, but unless readers have practiced the strategy successfully multiple times, they are unlikely to make the transfer to their independent reading. In this case, spend less time talking and more time reading!

If a reader is having difficulty using meaning as a source of information, you might say, "You already know that you can think about what's happening in the story to help you figure out or check a tricky word. Let's practice doing this." Then jump straight into the reading, coaching the child with prompts such as "Think about what's happening. Check it! Does it make sense?" You'll want to prompt only when necessary, to minimize interruptions and allow the child to do the work. When the child can use a strategy independently, hold him accountable for it. Make it clear you expect the reader to do this every time he reads, and make a note to check on the student's progress (and the effectiveness of your teaching) with another running record in a day or two.

Continue meeting with guided reading groups.

You will want to meet with your guided reading groups from yesterday again today. As described above, you may want to check in on the progress of these readers with a quick running record. Start the guided reading group by asking students to take out yesterday's book and read it independently. Listen in on one student and take a record of her first 100 words. While you won't have time to analyze the record right away, you should be able to check if the student is now reading the text at an independent reading level (96–100% accurate) and check for evidence of yesterdays' teaching point. Then reconvene the group to introduce and read a new, instructional-level text.

Readers, Like Editors, Listen and Fix Up Parts that Don't Sound Right

Invite children to listen to and check their own writing, fixing up sentences that don't sound right—just like editors do.

"As I moved around the room from reader to reader, I was so impressed with how carefully you were listening to your reading and checking that it sounded right. I thought, 'Boy! I sure wish there was a job where people had to read something and check if it sounded right, because the kids in *this* class would get hired in a second! And then it hit me! There *is* a job like that!" The students smiled back, wide-eyed. "Yes, there are people in the world whose job it is to do the same work you're doing! They are called *editors*. Editors read people's writing and listen carefully to make sure it sounds right. If it doesn't, they think, 'Hmm, . . . What *would* sound right here?' And they fix it up." I paused, looking up at the class with a sly smile. "So what do you say, *editors*? Are you up for the job?"

"Yeah!" shouted the class.

"Okay, you're hired. Let's do it! I'm going to pass out your writing folders and pens. Can you take out one of your stories and be an editor? First, read it and listen carefully. If it doesn't sound right, think, 'What kind of word should go next? What would fit?' And fix it up!" I coached in as kids edited their writing, prompting when necessary and saying, "Read that again and listen carefully," or "Listen to me read this line," rereading an incorrect sentence back to the child. "Did that sound right?"

"So remember, you can do this careful reading and listening work during reading workshop, *and* you can also do this same work during writing workshop. Whenever something doesn't sound right, you can fix it up!"

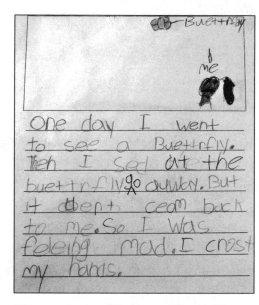

FIG. 7–2   As she edited her writing, Destiny, an English language learner, found a part that didn't quite "sound right" and added a word to fix the problem.

Readers Slow Down to Break Up Long Words

IN THIS SESSION, you'll remind readers to slow down to break up longer words part by part.

GETTING READY

✔ Make sure children are ready to bring white boards, markers, erasers and a book from their book baggies with them to the meeting area today (see Teaching and Active Engagement).

✔ Have magnetic letters nearby for building words (see Teaching and Active Engagement).

✔ Post the "Tools for Solving and Checking Hard Words" chart in the meeting area and have the new Post-it note—"Read it part by part"—ready to add. This will replace the "Look at ALL the parts of the word" Post-it (see Link)

✔ Post the "Be the Boss of Your Reading!" chart in the meeting area (see Mid-Workshop Teaching).

✔ Have a piece of chart paper ready so that you can interactively write a note to the principal with the students. (see Share).

MINILESSON

CONNECTION

Use a story to illustrate the idea of breaking up a difficult job, part by part.

"How many of you like to build with Legos?" The class burst out with excitement. "Well, when I was little, my brother and I used to play with Legos all the time! I would build a little house, and he would build something really hard, like a *big* castle, with tall walls, and watchtowers and even a bridge to cross a moat. I remember saying 'Whoa! I can't build anything like *that*. That's too hard!' But then my brother taught me something so important that I still remember it today. He said, 'It's actually not that hard, you just have to build it *part* by *part*.'

"You see, I was so busy looking at the *whole* castle, that I didn't think about the smaller parts. I could build walls and then add the towers and then add the bridge. Then, at the end I could step back, look at it all together and realize that I had an amazing castle, too.

"Readers, sometimes that same, 'Whoa! That's too hard!' feeling can happen when you read. Thumbs up if a tricky word in your book has made you feel that way. You might think, 'Whoa! I can't read a word like *that*!' Well, whenever that happens, remember the advice my brother gave me: It's not that hard. You just have to read it *part* by *part*!"

❖ Name the teaching point.

"Today I want to remind you that as your books get harder, some of the words also get harder. But you can slow down, look at all the parts of a word, and read it part by part."

TEACHING AND ACTIVE ENGAGEMENT

Use magnetic letters to build familiar words, and encourage children to break the words into known parts.

"Let's start by practicing this with some words and parts you already know. Ready?" I used magnetic letters to build the word *eat* on the easel, a word I had chosen from the class word wall.

"What's this word?"

Students responded confidently, "Eat!"

"Correct! I see vowels that go together." I separated the *t* to highlight the vowel pair, then I put the parts back together. "Now I'm going to add on to make this word longer." I added the inflectional ending *-ing* to the end of the word. "What's our new word?"

"Eating!" the children read in unison.

"Yes! This first part is *eat* and this last part is *ing*." I dramatically dragged the *eat* part to the left and then I pushed both parts back together while saying the word *eating*. "Let's try another one," I said.

I built another familiar word, this time using *jump* to make *jumping*. The class read it aloud, and I asked, "What are the parts? Can someone come up and show us?" I called on one child to separate the word *jump* from the *-ing* ending.

Encourage flexible word solving, prompting children to consider multiple ways to break a word into parts.

"Yes, that's one way to break the word into parts you see and know. Does anyone have a different way to break it? What are other parts you see and know?" I asked a few more children to come up and break the word in a variety of ways (e.g., j/ump/ing, j/umping, j/um/ping).

FIG. 8–1 Using magnetic letters to demonstrate different ways of breaking words part by part

Earlier in the year, your students learned to look at the beginning, middle, and end of a word (pl-ay-s) to read it accurately. Now that your readers are encountering more multisyllabic words, this job gets bigger. They will need to break words into more parts, and figure out how to read each of those parts (fan-tas-tic). To highlight this new work, you'll change the name of the strategy to say, "Read it part by part."

You'll want to use a known word so that the students can focus their attention on the concept you are trying to teach. Don't worry if this work seems too easy. Practicing with simple words will help students truly understand the concept and will make it more likely that they will be able to transfer the skill in their own reading.

Proficient readers problem solve words by working left to right across a word, breaking it part by part, not letter by letter. They also show a remarkable ability to be flexible in the way they do this. With this sequence of activities, you are teaching children not only to break words into parts, but also to be flexible in solving unknown words, encouraging students to consider multiple ways to break a word.

"Now, break this word into parts." This time, I built the familiar word *green*. Hands shot up to read the word. Then we worked, once again, to break the word into parts (e.g., /gr/een/, /gr/ee/n/).

"Let's see if you can tackle a bigger challenge. Ready?" The class agreed enthusiastically. I used the magnetic letters to construct the word *wonderful*—an unfamiliar word with parts that the children would know. "What parts do you see? Whisper to your partner."

I called a few students up to break the word into known parts, such as /won/der/ful/. "Let me read this word part by part. I can read the first part, /won/. Then the next part /der/. And the last part, /ful/. *Wonderful*!" I said, putting it all together.

Prompt students to write their own words for partners to read by using all the parts of the word.

"Right now, you try it. Look through one of your books for a word you can read. Write it down on your dry erase board. Then, see if your partner can figure out your word. Remind your partner to read across the word, part by part. You can use your finger to cover up some of the word to help you read each part." I moved around the meeting area to coach partners to consider different ways to break the words into parts, transferring their knowledge of word parts to increasingly more challenging words.

LINK

Encourage and support transfer by building children's confidence in their ability to use this strategy.

"Wow, readers! You know so many ways to solve hard words in your books. And now, thanks to all this practice with breaking words into parts, you are extra ready to use this tool with any bigger, harder words that get in your way. Remember, those words aren't so hard if you just read them part by part. You can use your finger to help read the first part, then the next part, and then the last part. Next, put it all together and keep on reading! You can try this strategy, along with all the other ones you know, any time you have to figure out a tricky word."

Ensure that you model different ways to break words into parts. In this minilesson, we've started with simple words that have inflectional endings (eating, jumping). These are generally the easiest types of words to break. We have also given students the opportunity to break a word into an onset and rime (green), as well as to work out the more challenging multisyllabic word, wonderful.

Add the new strategy to the chart, replacing the Post-it, "Look at all the parts of the word."

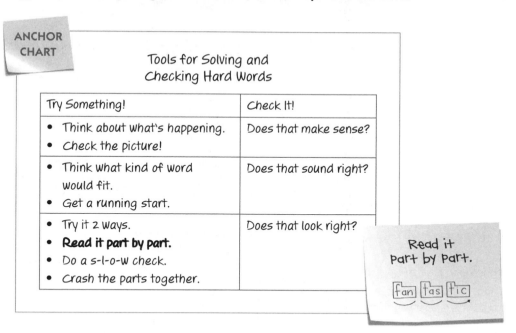

ANCHOR CHART

Tools for Solving and Checking Hard Words

Try Something!	Check It!
• Think about what's happening. • Check the picture!	Does that make sense?
• Think what kind of word would fit. • Get a running start.	Does that sound right?
• Try it 2 ways. • **Read it part by part.** • Do a s-l-o-w check. • Crash the parts together.	Does that look right?

Read it Part by Part.

fan tas tic

Good thing our "Caution: Readers at Readers at Work!" sign is up, because I can tell you're ready to get some big work done right now!"

FIG. 8–2   Students transition to their independent reading.

Supporting Independence in Word Solving

Meet with guided reading groups, lightening supports to give the readers more opportunities to solve challenges.

You will continue to divide your time between conferring and small-group work today, but you'll want to angle both toward a focus on supporting students to become more independent word solvers.

As you meet with the same guided reading groups for a third day, you will want to start to reduce scaffolds, simplifying your book introduction for today's new text, and leaving more challenges for the reader to tackle on her own. For example you might say, "This book is about a boy and his family going to the beach to fly a kite. Let's read and find out what happens at the beach." Then focus your attention on supporting children to problem solve as they read. You'll want this first reading to be successful, so consider carefully whether your students are ready for more independence with text at this level.

Work on taking words apart before, after, or while reading a text.

In both your small-group work and conferring you will want to make a decision about when to help students practice taking words apart. Proficient readers tend to decode words in larger parts, as opposed to letter by letter, and they can do it "on the run," without a lot of interruption to their reading. It's an important skill, so you'll want to take the time to help readers do this in the context of their books.

One possibility is before students read a text. Select a few multisyllabic words from a book and have children build these with magnetic letters. Then ask students to try reading the words by breaking them apart. Encourage these readers to try more than one way. You might coach them to recognize familiar spelling patterns, or break words into chunks that are easier to read, but don't jump in too quickly. If one way doesn't work, remind children to try it another way. They will need to have practice trying a word multiple times to persist at solving words in their own books. Make this practice

---

MID-WORKSHOP TEACHING
Readers Break Words in More Than One Way

"Readers," I said, standing beside our "Be the Boss of Your Reading!" chart and pointing to the first strategy. "Thumbs up if you stopped as soon as you noticed something was wrong and tried *something*?" The room filled with thumbs held up proudly in the air. "Double thumbs up if you tried to break a word, part by part, today." Many children indicated they had.

"Do you want to learn how to use this tool even better? Sometimes readers try to break up a word, part by part, but they still can't figure it out. When this happens, they don't give up!" I pointed to the next bullet on the chart. "You all know that a reader should try something and then something *else*. So here's the tip. If breaking up a word one way doesn't work, you don't have to try a whole different tool just yet. First, try to break it another way! Words can be broken in *lots* of different ways."

I quickly wrote the word *splatter* on the board in large letters and underlined parts of the word to illustrate how I might break it up. "I could break it like this" (spl att er). I erased the lines and redrew them. "Or like this" (spl atter). "Or like this!" (splatt er). "Splatt-er, splatter!" I said, demonstrating how to put the word together.

"But wait! There's one more step! Remember, when you think you've got it right, you have to . . ."

"Check it!" the class shouted enthusiastically.

"Okay readers, you've got this! Back to work!"

TRANSITION TO PARTNER TIME
Remind Partners to Use What They Know

"Readers," I said pointing to our partner chart, "You all know that one of the jobs you can do with your partners is to give them reminders. Here's another way to do that! You can remind your partners of everything they have learned about words and word parts. For example, one of our word study groups was learning about the word part, /ake/, and words like *make*. I bet if one of them got stuck on a word with that pattern, his partner could say, 'Hey! You know that part! You learned it in word study!'

"Readers, before we start our partner reading, could you turn to your partner right now and remind him or her of some of the word parts you know from word study?" I listened in as partners suggested word patterns such as /ight/ in *light* and vowel combinations such as /oa/ in *boat*.

"You know *a lot* about word parts! It's time to get going on reading your books together. Remember to help each other figure out tricky words, thinking about different ways to break up a word, and reminding your partners to use everything they know about how words work!"

short, as you are borrowing from the time children have to read continuous text. Then have children read the book you selected independently and watch to see how they tackle challenges. You could also have your readers select a few words to study after reading a text.

Alternatively, you could show kids how to take words apart while reading. When a child encounters a difficult word, you might say, "Use your finger to break it up. Read the first part. Look for something to help you. Now read the next part." To provide even more support you could have the reader quickly write the word on a Post-it or white board. Sometimes just this act of writing the word can help a reader to see and read the parts. Make sure the student then goes back to reread that section, putting the word back into context.

You'll want to keep in mind that readers should always be thinking about meaning as they work to decode words. Chances are that after reading the first part of the word, they will be able to predict the word by then thinking about what makes sense. Celebrate this efficiency—it's exactly what you want to see your readers doing! You may want to prompt the reader to "Check it!" quickly, making sure the last letters also match, and then get on with reading. Don't stop the reader for a long conversation to discuss the strategy. Instead, give the child more opportunities to practice this work.

Listening for Parts to *Write* Words

Connect the work readers do to decode, searching for parts to word solve, to the work writers do to encode, listening for parts to *spell*.

"I have a bit of news to share with you. Readers break words up, *looking* for parts they know to help them *read* words, and writers break words up, *listening* for parts they know to help them *write* words. You're working hard to do this in writing workshop so you can spell words the best you can. I'm wondering if we could practice a bit of that *writing* work to help us with this important *reading* work. What do you think? Let's try it!"

I clipped a fresh sheet of chart paper to the easel and suggested a topic for our interactive writing. "It might be nice to send the principal a note, perhaps inviting her to come visit our work zone! I am sure Ms. Park would be delighted if you showed her how you use all of your tools to read. What should it say? Turn to your partner and plan what we can write together." I moved around, listening for possibilities. I particularly searched for words that would help children practice breaking words into parts, including some that were multisyllabic and some with familiar patterns from word study. I gathered the group back together. "I heard so many suggestions. Maybe our note could say, 'We are working hard to do important reading jobs. Will you visit our classroom to see how we use powerful tools to help us read?'"

Prompt students to listen for each part of each word, clapping out longer words to hear each syllable, and then spelling the words in smaller parts.

"Let's write it. I'll start." I quickly recorded the first two words, because I wanted to concentrate our time on writing the longer words. "Now we need to write the next word, *working*. Will you say that word and listen for the parts? Now clap it! How many beats does *working* have?"

"Two!" shouted the class.

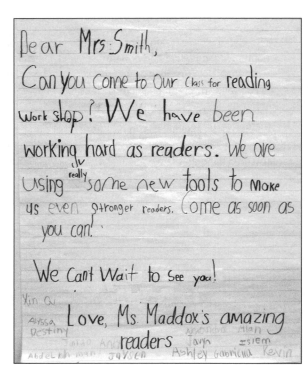

FIG. 8–3 Students use all they know about breaking a word into parts to write a letter to the principal.

"Let's listen to the first clap." I clapped my hands as I said the first part of the word. "*Work*. Let's write that. Say it slowly to help you!" I asked one child to record the letters on the chart paper, guiding her to use the part /or/ to record the sound in the middle of the word. I prompted the rest of the class to record the letters by tracing them on the rug, and again in the air. "Now let's do it with the next clap. Say the word and clap the beats again. What's the last part of the word?"

"*Ing*!" the class called back.

"Everyone, write the letters that make that ending. Sofia, come up and add them to spell *working* on the chart."

I reread from the beginning of the sentence. "We are working hard. That's the next word. Let's clap it." We said *hard*, clapping once. "Only one clap. That doesn't help us break it up. Let's say it slowly and think about the parts we hear."

The children said the word, stretching out each part. "I heard you break it into parts like this: /h/ /ar/ /d/. Let's write the first part," I said, recording the first letter. "What letters make up the next part, / ar/? Use what you know from your word work! Now write the last part."

I continued on, writing the short words myself and leading children through the process of breaking up longer words into parts and then writing each part. Once we had written the note, we reread it, using everything we know about word parts to check the spelling.

FIG. 8–4   As children have learned letter patterns in word study, they've sketched and added their own anchor words to match these patterns. You might use a resource like this one during interactive writing to help children transfer isolated word study to their reading and writing.

Readers Use Words They Know to Solve Words They Don't Know

IN THIS SESSION, you'll teach students to use the strategy of analogy, solving a new word by recalling one that looks similar.

GETTING READY

✔ Post the "Tools for Solving and Checking Hard Words" chart in the meeting area, and have the new strategy Post-it note—"Use a word you know"—ready to add (see Connection).

✔ Set students up to bring white boards, markers, and erasers to the rug (see Connection and Teaching and Active Engagement).

✔ Have your magnetic letters ready for making words (see Connection).

✔ Organize a pocket chart for sorting words into three columns, and prepare a set of index cards with words to be sorted (see Teaching and Active Engagement).

✔ Choose several places in your demonstration text for students to practice the work of the lesson. We chose the words *packed* on page 2 of *Zelda and Ivy*, *marched* on page 3, and *filled* on page 7. Leave these words uncovered (see Teaching and Active Engagement).

✔ Prepare a mini version of the "Tools for Solving and Checking Hard Words" and "Be the Boss of Your Reading" anchor charts for each child by printing the cover sheet (see Conferring and Small-Group Work).

✔ Create a small copy of your word wall to hand out to students (see Mid-Workshop Teaching).

✔ Obtain or create a letter from the principal or another visitor responding to yesterday's invitation from the class (see Share).

MINILESSON

CONNECTION

Channel kids to use known words to spell new words.

"Let's do a magic trick! Ready? Write the word *cat* at the top of your dry erase board. "The students quickly jotted the word down and held up their boards.

"Great!" I assembled the word in magnetic letters on the board for children to see.

"Now, hocus, pocus, alakazam! Turn your 'cat' into a 'hat'! Leave *cat* on your board and see if it can help you turn the word into *hat*." I watched as children replaced the first letter with an *h*. I assembled the word in magnetic letters under the first word. "If you know the words *cat* and *hat*, can you use more magic to turn your 'hat' into a 'splat'?" The kids worked as I observed carefully. Then, I used magnetic letters to build the word *splat*. "Abracadabra!" I announced, revealing the new word.

"That was fun! Let's try some more. Erase your boards!" I slid my first list of words to the side. "This time, write the word *stop* at the top of your board. Now turn the word *stop* into the word *stand*." I watched for students who wanted to match the ending, and voiced over a suggestion. "Think about which part of /st/op/ is the same as /st/and/. It might not be the ending! Say the words slowly to help you." I continued to assemble each word with magnetic letters so students were able to check their spelling. As kids recorded a new ending, I celebrated their work. "Voila! There it is, *stand*!

"Isn't it neat how knowing one word can help you write another word? Well, guess what? Using words you know doesn't just help you *write* new words. It also helps you *read* new words! How magical!"

✤ Name the teaching point.

"Today I want to teach you that readers can use words they *know* to read words they *don't know*. When you are stuck on a word, you can think, 'Do I know how to read or write a word that looks like this one?'"

TEACHING and ACTIVE ENGAGEMENT

Use known words to help kids make connections to new or unknown words by sorting them into columns on a pocket chart.

"Let's try this out together right now. I sat beside the pocket chart I had prepared and held up the first word, saying, "This words says . . ."

"Car!" the class called back. I placed the word *car* into the pocket chart, which made a header for the first column, before holding out the words *back* and *will* for the children to read. These words went at the top of the two remaining columns in the pocket chart.

"Readers, these are words we all know well. Now let's see if these words can help us to read some other words. I'm going to hold up a word. Even if you think you know it, please don't call it out. Instead, think, 'Is there another word up here,'" I pointed to the pocket chart, "'that could help me read this one?'"

I held up the first in a stack of index cards, with a large word printed on each. "Take a look at this word," I said, showing students the word *stack*. "Is there another word on the chart that could help you read it? Turn and quickly tell your partner."

I gave students just a few seconds to identify the word and called the class back. "I heard Ayan say that this word reminds her of the word *back*. If this says *back*," I said, pointing to the chart, "then this word says . . ."

"Stack!" the class shouted back. I repeated this process with the words *thrilling* and *sharpen*, making sure to remind kids to look all the way to the end of the word to figure out these more complex words.

FIG. 9–1 Words in a pocket chart for demonstrating the strategy of analogy

Readers use what they know in writing to help them problem solve when reading. Marie Clay emphasizes the reciprocal gains of reading and writing and how writing positively impacts a child's processing when reading. Explicitly teach children to use what they know in writing when they are reading and what they know in reading when they are writing.

You'll notice that this session begins with children trying out the strategy with words in isolation, before applying their learning in a book as well as a piece of shared reading (see Share). This supports readers in transferring the strategy to their own books independently.

Your aim for students will not just be to read the words on each index card, of course. Instead, you'll want to coach students to make connections between known words and new words, adding analogy to their repertoire of reading strategies.

"Wow! I'm amazed at how well you were able to figure out those words. It's almost like magic! Now let's see if we can do the same thing when we are reading words in a book."

Help students transfer this strategy to reading words in context.

"Let's go back to our book about Zelda and Ivy and see if we can use some of the words we know to help us read." I turned to page 2, placing the book under the document camera. "Here's the part where Zelda and Ivy decide to run away." I began to read, stopping at the highlighted word, *packed*.

> "*I'm coming too,*" said Ivy.
>
> She packed

I looked at the words on our pocket chart and back at the highlighted word in the text. "Readers, I think there's a word up here that can help us read this! Turn and tell your partner what word could help you." I gave students just a few seconds to identify the word *back* from the pocket chart.

"I heard lots of people say that this word is like *back*! If we know how to read *back*, I bet we can read the first part of this word." I used my hand to cover the last two letters in the word *packed*. "Read this first part with me. /P/ack/. *Pack*! Now let's read the last part." I lifted my hand to reveal the last letters and had students slowly read the whole word with me. "/Pack/ed/. Packed. Let's read from the beginning of the sentence and make sure it makes sense and sounds right, too. "'She *packed* her Princess Mimi doll, PJs, tea set, and Go Fish cards.' Yes! It makes sense, sounds right, and looks right!

"Let's try again!" We identified two more places for repeated practice with the strategy of analogy, using the word *car* to read *marched* on page 3, and *will* to read *filled* on page 7.

While we have identified several good places to try out the strategy of analogy, you may want to change the words you use to better meet the needs of your class. You could select places to highlight sight words your students have been working on or decide to reduce the complexity of the task, for example, using the word get *to read* set *on page 2.*

LINK

Connect the work readers and writers do to tackle new words, reminding children to use words they know.

"Did you realize we already have this tool on our writing chart? After all, you can use words you know to help you write words you don't know *and* now you can use words you know to help you read words you don't know. Wow, I think you'll probably want to use this tool during reading workshop *and* writing workshop. What do you think?" The class unanimously agreed.

Remind students to draw on all of their strategies for solving words, adding today's strategy to the chart.

"So, readers, from now on, remember that when you get stuck on a word, you have so many powerful tools to help you! You can take charge and use everything you know to get the job done. You can think about what would make sense." I gestured toward the meaning shelf on the chart. "You can think about what word would sound right." I gestured toward the syntax shelf on the chart. "And you can use the *whole* word to check all the parts. You can even think about a word you already know to help you read a new word." I pointed to the "Use a word you know." strategy that I had just added to the "Does it look right?" shelf of the chart.

Add to the chart.

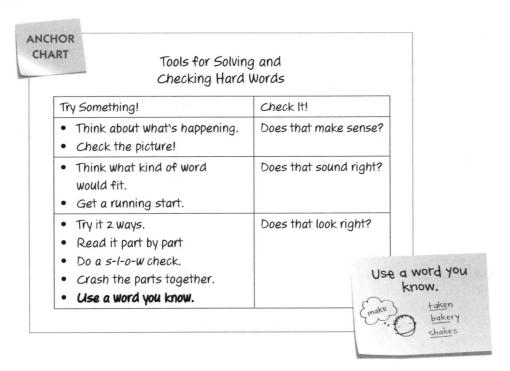

Supporting Independence in Reading

Meet with guided reading groups for a fourth day to support independence.

As you meet with your guided reading groups for the fourth day in a row, your goal will be to help students assume as much independence with this new level of text as possible. Instead of a book introduction today, you could ask students to take a sneak peek at the first half of the text and tell a partner what they think this book is going to be about.

Before kids start to read, be sure they have tools to support independence in reading. For example, they might have copies of the "Be the Boss of Your Reading" and "Tools for Solving and Checking Hard Words" charts (see online resources) as well as Post-its to write down troublesome unknown words in the text. You might then say, "Readers, today you are going to use everything you know to read this book on your own." You will, of course, jump in to support them if needed and give a teaching point at the end, but nonetheless, you have set the clear expectation that students will work with independence. Make careful observations, deciding if students are indeed ready to move to

reading this level of text independently or would benefit from additional small-group strategy work to support the transition.

Use coaching conferences to support students in using analogy to problem solve words.

As you confer with students today, you will want to spend some of your time helping them use analogy as a strategy for reading unknown words. This is a fairly complex

(continues)

MID-WORKSHOP TEACHING
Readers Can Use the Word Wall to Read Similar Words

"I want to give you a tip to help you recognize and figure out new words *in a snap*, just like you recognize and read words you know in a snap. You can read (and reread) the word wall to get those snap words fresh in your mind. That way, you can recognize similar words in your books and figure them out, in a snap. If you get stuck, you can think, 'Does that word look like a word I know? Is it just like a snap word I know?' I'll come around to give each of you a brand-new copy of our class word wall that you can add to your baggies. You can reread it to yourself. And if you get stuck in your book, check your copy of the word wall to see if there's a word that can help."

TRANSITION TO PARTNER TIME
Hunt for Words that Look Like Words You Know

"Readers, it's nearly time to meet with partners, and I thought of a game you might like to play. You already know that readers can hunt for word wall words in their books, but because you're such big-kid reading bosses now, I think you're ready to go on a more challenging hunt. What do you think? Are you up for a challenge?" The kids agreed enthusiastically.

"Great! You can work together, using your copies of the word wall, to hunt for words that *look* like words you know. Now, you'll need to keep your eyes alert and your minds sharp to spot them, because they're not always easy to find. If you spot a word before your partner, instead of just shouting it out, give clues. You can say, 'It's a word that looks like *jump*.' Or, you can say, 'I spy a word that looks like *make* but starts with /br/ and ends with an *s*.' Thumbs up if you think you might play this word hunt game today!" Many of the children signaled that they would. "After you hunt for words that *look* like words you know, be sure to spend time reading together. Your reading will be so much more powerful when you use words you know to figure out words that are new! Get started."

strategy that often requires some coaching to use successfully. For instance, have a child read aloud his text, and as he is reading, be on the lookout for words that lend themselves to this work. When the child comes to a challenging word, check to see if the word or any parts of the word are similar to a known word. For example, if the reader gets stuck on the word *dropped*, you might quickly write the word *stop* on a Post-it, saying "You know this word," and prompt the child by saying, "So now read the first part of this word," as you point back to the text. In essence, you are acting as the child's memory, cueing to known words that can be used as a helpful tool.

Remember, you can use analogy to read any part of a word, perhaps using *eat* to help read the middle of *scream*, or the word *tree* to help read *tricky*. You might even prompt a child to use two words to read a new word, perhaps using *she* and *make* to read the word *shakes*. You will not want to spend much time on lengthy explanations or demonstrations. Instead, prompt students to use the strategy in the moment and then continue reading. With successive opportunities to practice, they will be more likely to use the strategy independently.

After a little practice, reduce your level of support. Instead of providing a reader with a helpful word, you might instead say, "Do you know another word like that?" or "Can you write a word like that?" This puts the onus on the child to use the strategy with more independence. Keep in mind a child must have a fairly significant bank of known words to be able to apply this strategy independently. If students can't recall a similar word, this strategy will be difficult to use. Session 11 will help you work with children who need support expanding their knowledge of sight words.

You may, of course, decide to support students in using analogy within a small group. In this case, you might use a shared reading text to read together, stopping on highlighted words to practice the strategy together. Plan your strategy lesson carefully and give special consideration to the words you pick. It will not be helpful to demonstrate how the word *thought* helps you to read the word *brought*, unless *thought* is a well-known word for all the children in your group. Remember, you are teaching the principle of this word-solving strategy, not simply trying to solve the words in the text you select. It will be more helpful to have children use a well-known word like *new* to read *grew*, or *car* to figure out the word *sparkle*.

Using New Tools to Read New Words

Share a letter from the principal, or someone else in the school, who has agreed to come visit your classroom to learn about the tools students are using as readers.

As soon as the class had settled back in the meeting area, I held up a rolled piece of chart paper, tied with a string. "You'll never believe it! The principal got our note and wrote us back. Shall we read it together?" The class cheered, anxious to read the letter. I unrolled the paper and clipped it to the easel. I had highlighted several words in the letter to prompt the class to solve words part by part and to use analogy as well. "Oh my! It looks like some of the words are highlighted. I think Ms. Park wants us to do some work to figure out those tougher, longer words. Do you think we can do it? Let's read together, and when we get to a highlighted word, let's stop and use our tools to solve it." I invited the class to read along with me.

Read the letter with the class, stopping at highlighted words to prompt children to break them into parts or to use word analogies, drawing on familiar words to read unfamiliar words.

> Dear Class 1A,
>
> I am so happy to hear about the `fantastic` reading jobs you are doing.

I stopped at the first highlighted word in the text, *fantastic*. "This a pretty long word. Remember the tool you have to tackle words that feel too big. Break it up and read it part by part." I gestured toward the chart. "Even if you know this word, turn and tell your partner what parts you see." I listened in and, after a brief moment, called students back to break the word together. "Many of you saw this first part, /fan/. Let me break the next part, I see /tas/. Let's all say the last part." I pointed under the ending of the word, as the kids read /tic/. "Now, I said, "put the parts together to say the word." I slid my finger under the word as the children read aloud. "*Fantastic!*" We reread the line and moved to the next sentence:

> Every time I see the sign outside your door, it reminds me that the first grade is hard at work. I `would` love to come and visit. I am excited to learn all about the `many` tools you use to read!
>
> Your proud principal,
>
> Ms. Park

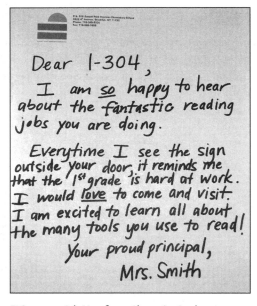

FIG. 9–2   A letter from the principal responding to an invitation the children sent

I paused at the word *would*. "Hmm, . . . let me see if I can break this word into parts." I mouthed several chunks, demonstrating a struggle. "I don't know if this tool is going to help me here. Luckily, we have *another* tool that can help. We can use a word we know. Does this word look like another word you know? Check the word wall!" Kids quickly raised their hands to volunteer the word *could*. "Yes! I bet that can help us read this word. Read it with me." The students filled in *would* and we read on, stopping again to connect the word wall word *any* to read *many* .

"How exciting! Ms. Park will be coming to learn about our work! You'll need to keep those tools of yours powered up. Remember that when you get to words that feel tough, you can break them up and read them part by part. You can also think of a word you know! If one tool doesn't work, try another!"

FIG. 9–3   Jenna uses a word she knows to help her figure out a new word in her book.

Readers Try Sounds Many Ways to Figure Out Words

Try it many ways.

beak   food

pear   book

heart   door

MINILESSON

In your connection, harken back to the work students did to learn the sounds of long and short vowels. You might say, "Earlier this year you learned that vowels can make two sounds, and you've gotten so good at trying them two ways. You see, some sounds are sneaky. They're sometimes in disguise because they don't *look* the way they *sound*. Vowels aren't the only sneaky sounds. Sometimes a whole group of letters will team up, and it's your job to figure them out. You can say the word or the word part a bunch of different ways to figure it out."

Then, name the teaching point. Say, "Today I want to teach you that readers are flexible. They know that letters and groups of letters can make different sounds. You can say the word or the word part many ways to figure it out." Then, add the strategy Post-it note—"Try it many ways"—to your "Hard Words" anchor chart, replacing "Try it two ways" to refine the tool for your growing readers.

In your teaching, you'll want to demonstrate this work explicitly. Urge the children to watch and listen carefully as you approach a "tricky" word in your book. You might say, "Hmm, . . . this is a hard word. Let me slide my finger under it to say the sounds one way and listen to check that it sounds right and makes sense." You might turn to page 4 of *Zelda and Ivy: The Runaways*, placing it under the document camera. Read aloud and stop at the word *spread*. Then move across the word, pronouncing the letters as they look: /spr/ee/d/. Then, stop to monitor meaning and syntax. "That's not quite right. Let me try again. I bet there are some sneaky sounds hiding here." Then, move back across the word, rereading to say it a few different ways before pronouncing the word correctly. "Oh! *Spread*! That's it. That makes sense and sounds right here."

In your active engagement, you might choose to read to the first line of page 8, stopping at the word *fourteen* and pronouncing it a few different ways, such as /fo/er/ teen/ and /f/ow/r/teen/. Then ask the kids if either of those sound right. The children are surely bound to shake their heads, while some will read the word automatically. This work is not about identifying the word, but is about reinforcing the mind-set that readers need to be flexible, trying the words a few different ways. "What sneaky sounds are hiding here? This word certainly doesn't *look* the way it *sounds*." Prompt partners to identify the word parts that are making a sound unlike the letters in the pattern. In this instance, the *ou*, as in *your*, sound in the pattern /ou/.

Link today's work with the ongoing job readers have: to stop when something's not quite right and try *something* to fix it up. Remind children to add this tool to their toolboxes to help them when there are sneaky sounds hiding in the words in their books.

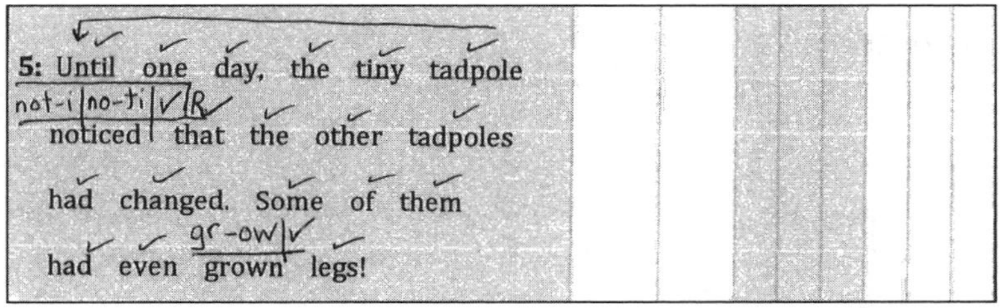

FIG. 10–1   As children begin to solve more complex words you'll want to see evidence of flexible problem solving. Here a student tries a word in several different ways and rereads to check that it makes sense.

CONFERRING AND SMALL-GROUP WORK

In your conferences and small groups, you might choose to pull together children who need more support studying word parts in isolation. You could do some small-group word study to explore word patterns, coaching kids to see, say, and sort similar words to support flexibility with sounds. For example, you might sort words with the /ea/ sound, as in words like *bean* and *leap*, as well as the sound in *pear* and *head*. Have children reflect on how they sorted the words to develop an understanding of the principle.

Mid-Workshop Teaching

In your mid-workshop teaching, take some time to refer children back to any word study charts or tools in the room to refresh their minds about the vowel combinations they have learned in isolation, as a way to support transfer. Remind students to use these patterns to help them make the sounds as they decode unknown words in their books. You might say, "Remember, you learned some tricky patterns like *oo*. Sometimes two *os* make /oo/ like in *food*, but sometimes it sounds like /oo/ in *book*. You also know that words can end with *-ed*, but sometimes the ending sounds more like /t/, as in *jumped*. Be sure to try it a few ways to listen for the word that sounds right and makes sense."

FIG. 10–2   Here the class has collected and celebrated words they've tried different ways.

Transition to Partner Time

As you transition to partner time today, suggest that children share any words with sneaky sounds that they may have discovered in their reading. Encourage children to record a few examples on Post-its to share with their partners. You might even create an interactive chart in your classroom, perhaps titled, "Caught You! Sneaky Sounds in Our Books" and invite students to add their words.

SHARE

During your share, inspire children to be curious about words. You might say, "We can learn more about words and how they work every time we read by studying words closely and with a curious mind." You might choose to collect students' words on an interactive chart, taking a moment to study a few examples together. Say, "Let's look at this word: *tough* (on page 8 of *Zelda and Ivy*). Read it with me. Listen to the sound at the end, /f/. What letters are making that sound? Have we seen any other words like that (*laughing*, on page 11)?" Children might even look back at the interactive chart during writing workshop to support spelling words when they don't look quite right, thinking, "Is that the way it would look in a book? Let me try to spell it another way."

Readers Use Sight Words to Read Fluently

MINILESSON

IN THIS SESSION, you'll remind students to read sight words in continuous text fluently, and to expand their repertoire of known words by rereading.

CONNECTION

Guide students in an inquiry to notice and name some of the word-solving tools they've learned throughout this bend.

"Today we're going to do a little investigation. Put on your detective hats!" I put on my own hat as the kids followed suit. "I'm going to read a page and, as I read, can you listen carefully and try to name the tools I use to solve tricky words? Collect them on your detective pads." I held out my palm, pretending to record notes with an imaginary pen. "Use our chart to help you remember!"

Holding the book in my lap, rather than under the document camera, I began reading from page 12 and modeled several word-solving strategies. "'Pretty soon salsa music–'" I looked up, furrowing my brow, as if stuck. "Let me read the first part," I said to myself, putting my finger into the text. "Dr/if/ted/. Drifted!" I continued reading, modeling a few more strategies, including slowly working through a couple of words that I knew the children would easily recognize (*out, home*). After another minute, I set the book down. "Okay, detectives, quickly turn and talk to your partner. List all the tools I used to solve words!"

Remind readers that they have been learning words for a long time and they now have a large bank of words they can read in a snap.

"Wow, you noticed so many tools. Good detective work!" I exclaimed. I made my face serious, paused, and took a deep breath. "Well, it's true. I *did* use lots of tools to take charge of my reading, and I worked hard to figure out those tough words. But now that I think about it, I'm not sure I really needed to solve all those words. Like this one." I placed page 12 under the document camera and pointed to the word *out*. "We know this word says . . ."

"Out!" shouted the class.

"Yes! I didn't need to figure *that* out. I already know it! And you know a *lot* of words you can read in a snap!" I gestured to the word wall. "Remember when we read our word wall words to help us read new words a couple of days ago? Well, that was a reminder that you *do* know a lot of words! In fact, you've been using a word wall as a tool to help you remember words since you were in kindergarten. But now that you are in first grade, that tool is *way* bigger. There are so many more words on it!

"But that's not the only place you've learned new words! You've also learned words from the books you've been reading." I placed pages 12 and 13 back under the document camera. "For example," I said, pointing to the words, "we know how to read the words *sisters* and *fox* and the names *Ivy* and *Zelda* in a snap because they're all through the pages of this book. You won't need to stop and figure out these words each time you see them! There are *lots* of words you already know how to read!"

FIG. 11–1 Students warm up for their independent reading by reading the word wall.

❖ **Name the teaching point.**

"Today I want to remind you that readers only slow down to read a word when they *have* to. Instead, they read most of the words in their books in a snap and keep on going, making their reading as smooth as it can be."

TEACHING

Recruit students to help you monitor your reading for words you should recognize and read fluently.

"Now, will you watch me carefully as I read a page in our book? Check to see if I'm reading the words I know in a snap, making my reading nice and smooth. If so, give me a thumbs up. I might have to slow down a little to read a word I don't know, and that's okay. But if I stop on a word I should read in a snap, please let me know! Tap your finger on the side of your head to remind me that I should be able to remember that word." I began reading from page 12, first reading fluently, with the occasional pause to quickly solve a word.

I stopped at the word *love* and feigned confusion. I furrowed my brow and, with great concentration, began to break the word part by part. "/L/oov/. /Low/v/" I shook my head and looked up to see the class smiling and tapping the side of their heads. "Huh?" I said, sounding surprised. "You think I know this word and can read it in a snap?! Let me look again." I went back and reread the prior sentence. "'I bet they're dancing,' said Ivy. 'I sure LOVE to dance.'"

"Oh." I said sheepishly. "You were right! I definitely did *not* need to slow down to figure out that word. I could have read that whole part nice and smoothly if I was watching out for the words I know.

"Let me try again." I continued reading from page 13 to the end of the chapter, slowing only once or twice to look carefully. With a shake of the head I said, "Nope. Don't know that word," before quickly solving it and reading on fluently. I looked up at the class to see students holding up their thumbs to signal, "That was way better!"

Make sure students are referencing your updated word wall and using it as a reminder of the words they know and can read with ease.

ACTIVE ENGAGEMENT

Set students up to coach each other, watching out for words they know and can read quickly.

"Now it's your turn! Partner 1, get your book out and quickly choose a part to read. Partner 2, it's your job to help out by being a second set of eyes and ears. Watch carefully, and if you notice your partners slowing down for words they know, give them a little reminder to read them in a snap and keep on going, making their reading as smooth as it can be. "Go ahead!" As students started reading, I quickly listened in to a few partnerships.

"I'm hearing some smooth reading!" I voiced over, as an encouragement. "Make sure you only slow down when you *have* to," I prompted. "Remember, you know almost all of these words already!"

After a few minutes, I pulled the group back together and highlighted the work of one partnership. "Readers, I heard lots of nice, smooth reading. Jenna was reading words she knows as quick as a blink! She did have to stop and figure out the word *window*, but guess what? When she saw that word again on the next page she didn't stop. This time, she just read it in a snap! Her partner didn't even have to remind her; she just took charge of her reading and only slowed down when she really needed to."

LINK

"Readers, you know how to figure out new words, and you have so many tools for doing this. But don't forget that no matter what book you read today, tomorrow, or even next week, there are going to be *lots* of words that you already know. Watch out for those words and read them in a . . ." I trailed off so the class could chime in.

"Snap!" they shouted.

"You got it!" I laughed. "Remember, reading the words you know quickly will keep your reading sounding nice and smooth. Only slow down to solve a word if you *have* to. Let's add that to our chart of tools so we don't forget." I added the strategy "Check if it's a snap word." to our "Tools for Solving and Checking Hard Words" chart.

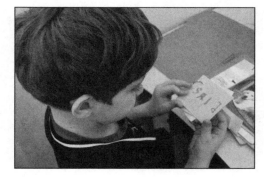

FIG. 11–2 Islem reads his ring of sight words to remind himself of the words he should be able to read in a snap.

Taking Stock

Use the anchor chart to assess readers' knowledge of the strategies taught across this bend.

Now that you're at the end of the second bend, you'll want to take stock of your readers' ability to problem solve. You can use a small version of the "Tools for Solving and Checking Hard Words" anchor chart to do this (see online resources 👆). As you move from student to student today, watch for *how* they are solving words. After listening in on a child read a page or two, you might stop her and ask a few questions to better understand what she does when problem solving. In some cases it will be obvious, particularly when she breaks a word part by part or gets a running start, but much of this work will have happened internally. You might then ask the child, "Tell me how you figured this out." Show genuine interest, and listen carefully to learn as much as you can about the way she approaches difficult words. Remember, you typically

wouldn't want to interrupt children's reading for lengthy conversations about their problem solving; but in this case you're informally assessing their understanding of the strategies you taught in this bend.

When you observe and talk to a child, you might keep a tally of each time you notice a strategy being used, putting a hash mark beside the strategy on the child's small version of the anchor chart. Use the chart to determine strengths and next steps. You could then give the child a compliment, perhaps saying, "Wow! You've become a real expert at figuring out different ways to break a word part by part! Nice job working hard to use that tool!" Then remind the child of a strategy he is neglecting to use that would be helpful. "There is another very helpful tool that you're not using very often yet. Remember, you can also think about what's happening in the story to help you

(continues)

MID-WORKSHOP TEACHING   **Remembering Known Words**

"Readers, I'm noticing something really interesting as you're reading. I've seen a few people stop on a word and say, 'Wait, wait, I know this word! Um . . .'" I held my head with two hands, acting like a person who is trying hard to remember something. "Um . . . I know it! I know it! I've seen it in *lots* of my books. I just can't remember it!'" I threw my hands up in frustration.

"Has that ever happened to you?" A few heads nodded in agreement. "Well, *you* are the boss of your reading! You can do something about it! First, use all your tools to figure it out. Then, if you know it's a word you've seen again and again, not just in this book, but in lots of books, write it down." I quickly modeled writing the word *through* on a Post-it. "This word says, 'through.' If you have a hard time remembering it, you can use the Post-it as a reminder to teach it to yourself. Then, during word

study or at home, or whenever you have an extra minute, you can turn that word into a snap word so you'll know it whenever you see it!

"You can look at it, say it, spell it, write it, and then check it, just like we do with our word wall words. You can practice writing it on a dry erase board and see how fast you are. You can make it with magnetic letters and read it. You can even put it on a little card to keep in your pocket and practice reading it wherever you go! You can teach yourself the words you need to know.

"Readers, as you go back to your reading, watch out for these words. Don't let them stump you! Be the boss and make yourself a little reminder on a Post-it to learn them!"

"Readers, a very special guest has arrived!" I opened the door to invite the school principal into the room. "Ms. Park, we are so glad you're here to see how much we've learned!" The principal told the children a little bit about how she had noticed them working so hard every time she passed by the classroom and was excited to hear about the reading jobs they had learned to do.

"So, readers, now is your chance to show off how powerful your reading has become. First, let's read our 'Tools for Solving and Checking Hard Words,' chart for Ms. Park to teach her about the powerful reading tools you have and the important jobs you do when you read!" We read the chart together. "Readers, Ms. Park is excited to come around while you are reading and working with your partners so she can watch you in action—taking charge of your reading!"

As the students read together, Ms. Park sailed around the room, listening into partnerships and giving them each a compliment. At the end of partner time, Ms. Park thanked the class. "Wow, that 'Caution! Readers at work!' sign on your door is right; this is a room *full* of readers hard at work! Keep it up!"

It is critical that readers have a large bank of sight words to support fluency and to use as a tool for problem solving through analogy. You might start by building a word with magnetic letters. Read it to the children and then pass them their own set of letters to build the word from left to right. Then have them mix up the letters and build the word again several times. Next have the children practice writing the word on their dry erase boards. Then, cover the model and have students write the word on their own, before revealing the model and prompting children to check, editing their spelling if necessary. As students practice writing the word, prompt them to write it quickly, so that it becomes an automatic response. You may even have students get up to write the word in giant letters on the board, moving their entire body as they do this.

You might move on to repeat this process with two or three other words. Then give each child a text at his or her independent reading level featuring some of the words you've practiced and have the students read, watching out for these new words. After reading, have the children close their eyes and "see" the words in their brains. Remind them that they will need these words later in the day and tomorrow—and anytime they read or write! As you send them off, you may want to write the words on index cards and have students add them to their word rings for future reference.

Monitor these children closely, keeping track of the sight words they know so you can hold them accountable for recognizing and reading those words in their texts. Consider keeping a list of sight words that the children in this group know, and use it for reference when prompting students as they read, ensuring that they will read these words in a snap and use them to read unknown words through analogy.

figure out a hard word. Why don't you try that in your book right now?" Then coach the child to apply the strategy.

Help readers add to their personal word banks.

When conferring today, you may also want to work with kids who have trouble learning and remembering new words. Identify these children by taking a look at your high-frequency word assessments to see who would benefit from small-group work.

Checking in and Setting New Goals

Celebrate students' growth as readers, having learned how to use enough tools to fill a whole tool shed!

I gathered students back in the meeting area. As the children found their spots beside partners, I clipped the "Tools for Solving and Checking Hard Words" chart to the easel. "I am so impressed with the tools you've learned to use as readers. You are working so hard to get the job done, stopping to solve hard words and check your reading. It's almost like we've filled a whole tool shed!"

I gestured toward the chart. "Right now, I'm going to give each of you your own toolbox." I held up a mini-chart, distributing a final copy of the class anchor chart to each child. "Well, not a *real* toolbox." I smiled. "But now you'll have your own copy of the chart and your own set of reading tools to help you fix up your reading and get the job done."

Rally students to use the chart to reflect on strategies they've learned. Then, prompt partners to work together to set a goal.

Once every student had a copy, I continued. "Now that you are stronger, tougher, more powerful readers, I think it's time to check in with your reading and set a new goal. You can study each tool in your toolbox and think, 'Is this a strategy I use *all* the time? Or is this something I need to push myself to try *more* often?' Then, you can set a goal for yourself; after all, you're in charge of your own reading. So right now, work with your partner to decide what strategies you use *all* the time and what strategies you'll set a goal to use *more*. Get to it, bosses!"

I moved around the rug to listen in, guiding students toward appropriate goals when necessary. I handed each student a star sticker to mark the strategy they'd plan to use more often, helping make their goals more tangible.

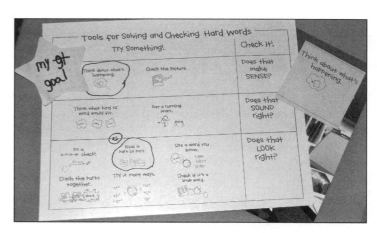

FIG. 11–3 Nima reflects on her reading. She marks "Read it part by part" as the strategy she uses all the time with a smiley face and places a star next to her goal, "Think about what's happening."

Readers Work to Understand, Rereading If They Don't Get It

IN THIS SESSION, you'll teach students to monitor for meaning not only when they're solving words, but also as they read across whole parts of longer, more challenging books, checking to make sure they understand each part of what they read, and rereading when they don't get it.

GETTING READY

✔ Choose a demonstration text at, or slightly above, the current benchmark level to use throughout the third bend. We use Chapter 2 in *Zelda and Ivy: The Runaways* (see Teaching and Active Engagement).

✔ Mark the demonstration text in a few places to stop and think with the students, "Am I getting it?" We suggest pages 17 and 24 in *Zelda and Ivy* (see Teaching and Active Engagement).

✔ Prepare a new chart titled "Tools for Understanding Our Books" and have the first strategy Post-it note—"Check that you're getting it!"—ready to add (see Link).

✔ Display the "Reading Partners Work Together" chart and have the new Post-it note—"We think, 'What might happen next?'"—ready to add (see Share).

MINILESSON

CONNECTION

Challenge your readers not only to figure out tricky words, but also to take on the job of *understanding* longer, more challenging books.

"Yesterday, as I was moving from person to person and listening in on all your great reading work, I noticed something about the books you're reading. Your books look a *lot* different from the ones you were reading at the beginning of first grade. Have you noticed that, too?" The children nodded proudly. "*These* books are way harder than the books you used to read! But you're taking charge—using all your tools to get the job done—solving words and checking your reading. Nice work!

"But here's the thing. Figuring out the words is only *one* of your jobs as a reader. Readers actually have a way *bigger* and more *important* job to do." I paused, building anticipation for the work ahead. "Readers must *always*—*every* time they read—work hard to *understand* their books. And if you are going to continue to read harder and harder books, then you are going to need new tools to help you get the job done."

❖ **Name the teaching point.**

"Today I want to teach you that readers don't just work hard to read *words*. They work hard to understand their *books*. As you read, *always* check, 'Am I getting it?' If not, reread to figure out how everything fits together."

TEACHING AND ACTIVE ENGAGEMENT

Give students several opportunities to monitor for understanding and to reread to clarify thinking.

"Let's try this together." I put the book *Zelda and Ivy: The Runaways* under the document camera, opening to the second chapter. I read the title. "'The Time Capsule.' Hmm, . . . I wonder what that's about? Let's read and find out." We read through page 17 together and I paused to collect my thoughts, feigning confusion. "I feel like Zelda just told us what a time capsule is. I think it has something to do with this container," I said, pointing to the picture. "Hmm, . . . Let me check. 'Am I getting it?' I'm not so sure. I'm still a little confused. I need to reread and try to really *understand* what's happening." I reread the page a second time. "Okay, turn and talk. What do you understand so far?"

I listened in, quickly assessing students' ability to draw meaning from a short piece of text. When I heard some students using their background knowledge to talk about a time capsule, I asked them to confirm their ideas with the text. "You can use the words in the book to help you explain your thinking," I voiced over. Then I brought the group together.

"Readers, you sure are trying to understand your reading the best you can. I saw Michael going back to read this page *again*, and then he said that he thinks Zelda is making some sort of present because she wrote 'A gift' on the container, and he knows that *gift* means the same as *present*. I also heard Judy say that she thinks this gift is for someone in the future, a long time from now. But Judy said she wasn't really sure what was in it. I agree with her. I don't know what is in the present either."

"Maybe it's that jewel in the picture!" called Eric.

"It could be. Let's keep reading and see if we can understand even more about what's going on. Read with me." I invited the children to read along with me, and we continued on to the end of page 21 before stopping to check in. "Okay, readers, are we getting it? Do we understand what's happening now? Turn and talk. Tell your partner everything you know so far." As I listened to students clarifying their thinking this second time, I paid careful attention to misunderstandings or disagreements that could be cleared up with some rereading.

"Wait a second, readers!" I interrupted. "I'm hearing some people say that this present might be for Zelda's friends to find. Let's check if we're getting it. Then we can reread to see if we can understand that better." We reread page 18, stopping after the second sentence. "Oh! Did you get that? Zelda said, 'A *hundred* years from now, someone will open this box and find my lucky jewel.' I don't think this present is for her friends. I think this present is for someone to find in 100 years! That's a *long* time in the future! Good thing we checked if we were getting it and reread to really understand what was going on."

We then read three more pages, stopping at page 24 to monitor for understanding once more. "Wait. What's going on? I'm confused. Why is Mimi the *only* thing in the time capsule? Wasn't there other stuff in there as well? I don't get it. What should we do?" I prodded.

"Reread!" the class called back.

You'll notice that you're starting with a small chunk of text. By doing so, you can demonstrate that reading for meaning involves lingering over text and doing a lot of thinking along the way. Help your students learn to approach text with a tentative frame of mind, saying, "I think what's going on is . . ." so they will not be afraid to slow down and reread to clarify, confirm, or revise an idea.

While these are examples of how students might monitor for meaning while reading the text, you will want to follow your students' lead. Listen carefully for confusion or misconceptions, and reread to explore these ideas, giving kids an authentic context for checking their understanding.

"That's right!" We flipped back to pages 18 and 19 to confirm that there were two items in the box. Then, partners discussed why the box might be empty now to clarify understanding, before coming back together as a class.

LINK

Debrief, adding the strategy to a new anchor chart that shows the comprehension tools readers can use to support understanding of their books.

"I can already tell that you're the kind of readers who don't just work hard to *read* words. You also work hard to *understand* your books. So remember, whenever you read, you *always* need to check, 'Am I getting it?' And if you're not, then . . ."

"Reread!" the class chimed in.

"Yes, go back and reread to figure out how everything fits together. Let's add this tool to our new chart. We'll fill *this* toolbox with strategies that can help us *understand* our books." I added the strategy Post-it note to the chart and transitioned kids into independent reading.

ANCHOR CHART

Tools for Understanding Our Books

• Check that you're getting it!

Supporting Students in Reading for Meaning

Emphasize the work of reading for meaning.

During your conferring and small-group work today, you will want to turn an eye toward comprehension. With the emphasis on word solving in the previous bends, you will not want students becoming preoccupied with text at the word level. Conduct some quick table conferences to encourage reading for meaning.

You might start by observing a child at one table, watching to see if she stops to monitor for meaning and then rereads to clarify an idea. To get a better sense of this, ask a few research questions, such as "What's going on in your book?" or "What is this book making you think right now? Why?" You will want to listen carefully to check that the student has a strong understanding of the text and is acting with initiative when uncertain. If not, steer the child in this direction, perhaps pretending to be confused and saying, "Wait, I'm not getting this. Are you? Why don't you read that again

to understand it better." Then celebrate this accomplishment, acting as if it was the child's idea all along. Do not only compliment the child, but interrupt the entire table to share the great reading work that just happened. In this way, not only is it more likely that one child will repeat this behavior, but you will have recruited a whole group of others to do the same!

Design a series of small groups to teach across the next couple of days, taking into consideration the needs of your higher-level readers.

As you move fully into this bend, you will want to make some decisions about the small groups you'll be meeting with. You'll likely want to get another series of guided reading groups started. This would also be a good time to support your stronger readers.

Before you meet with your higher-level readers, though, look through their books to understand the challenges they'll be facing. While many early chapter books tend to be

(continues)

MID-WORKSHOP TEACHING
Remembering to Read Smoothly

"Readers, when you read, it's important to listen to yourself. When your reading voice is smooth, it's easier to understand what's happening. But when you stop to fix up words, your reading begins to sound bumpy and boring! When this happens, it's easy to get confused about what's happening. So here's a tip. Go back to the bumpy parts and reread to smooth them out. This not only helps your reading voice sound better, but it also helps you *understand* the story better.

"Can you take a look at your book right now and find a spot that got a little bumpy? Now reread it smoothly, paying careful attention so you'll understand *exactly* what's going on."

TRANSITION TO PARTNER TIME
Getting Help to Understand Confusing Parts

"Readers, it is just about time to meet with your partner! You already have gotten so good at working together to fix up tricky words. But did you know that's not the only type of problem a partner can help you fix up? Partners are also great at helping each other fix up confusing parts. I'm going to give you a special colored Post-it in a minute. If you have a place where you are confused about something, or are wondering what's going on, mark it with the Post-it. Then you can explain what you *think* is happening, and say 'But I'm not sure about . . .' and explain why you are confused. Then, together you can reread to *understand* that part of the story better."

---

episodic, with a new little story in each chapter, others carry the story across chapters, requiring the reader to track events and maintain meaning over longer periods of time. In addition, your stronger readers may be dealing with texts that have more dialogue, a higher frequency of pronouns for the reader to keep track of, more scene and time changes, and new vocabulary. Select a challenge to address and design some small-group work around this area.

For example, you might pull together a few students and say, "I've brought you together because now that you're reading harder books, it's even more important to check that you're getting it. You see, in the books you are reading now, characters don't always stay in the same time and place. In fact, in some of your books, the story happens over many days and in many places! If you don't keep track of this, your books may start to get really confusing. The good news is that authors give you clues to help you know about changes in time or place. They might use words like *the next morning* or *later that day* or *when she got to the store* to let you know that the time or place has changed. Let's practice this right now. Start reading your books and watch out for these clues to help *understand* your books better. When you see one, pause and check, 'Where and when is this happening?' to track the story."

You may coach children as they practice this in their own books, or you might decide to give students a new book to read with a partner. Students could hunt for these phrases while reading, perhaps using highlighter tape to mark them, and then pause to clarify the change in scene and time. Make sure they leave the group understanding that this work can continue in all the books they read.

Think, "What's Next?" to Understand More

Have students play reporter again, this time asking each other what might happen next.

"Readers, I have an idea for a way to check that you're getting it when you read with your partners. You can play 'This Just In!' Only this time, the reporter isn't just going to say what's happened. The reporter is also going to interview his or her partner and ask, 'What do you think is going to happen *next*?' Let's try it together. I'm going to be the reporter, and will you all be my partner?" The class eagerly agreed. I held an imaginary microphone up to my mouth and clasped my earpiece with my other hand. "This just in! We have an update on Zelda and Ivy's time capsule. Ivy just snuck over to the cherry tree and dug up the time capsule. But when she looked inside, she only saw her doll Mimi! We know from looking at the facts that there were *two* objects in the time capsule! This is very strange! Partner 2, what do you think is going to happen *next*?" I looked out at the hands waving and leaned over to hold the microphone in front of a student.

"I think Zelda and Ivy will see a hole in the capsule and find out that the jewel is lost," Ayan predicted.

I moved my microphone to another student. "I think that Ivy will find out that Zelda took her jewel back but didn't tell her! Zelda wants it to help her play the piano," suggested Anthony.

"We don't know why the capsule is empty yet, but there are two ideas about what might happen *next*. Stay tuned for further updates. Back to you, Partner 2!" I put down my microphone.

"Readers, thinking about what might happen next can help you understand even more about your books. And playing reporter is a fun way to practice that! Will you quickly turn to your partner and take out your microphones and ask, "What do *you* think will happen *next*?" I gave students a little time to share their predictions and then brought the class together.

"Are you ready to check? Let's read the next two pages very carefully and work hard to *understand* how this chapter ends." We finished reading the chapter as a shared reading to check our predictions. Afterward, I added this strategy to our partner chart.

ANCHOR CHART

Reading Partners Work Together

- We give reminders.
- We grow ideas together.
- We give book introductions.
- We don't just tell—we HELP!
- We do SOMETHING at the end.
- We work together to solve hard problems.
- We keep track of what's happening.
- **We think, "What might happen next?"**

We think, "What might happen next?"

Readers Make Mind Movies to Picture What's Happening

IN THIS SESSION, you'll teach children to envision the scene as they read, using the pictures and the words to make a movie in their mind.

GETTING READY

✔ Display the chart "Tools for Understanding Our Books" in the meeting area and have the new strategy Post-it note—"Make a movie to picture what's happening."—ready to add (see Connection and Share). ✋

✔ Choose a place in your demonstration text to use for modeling and student practice. We use pages 20–24 in Chapter 2 of *Zelda and Ivy: The Runaways* (see Teaching).

✔ Have ready the "Reading Partners Work Together" chart and the new strategy Post-it note—"We act it out to understand."—ready to add (see Transition to Partner Time). ✋

✔ Set children up to bring their goal-setting sheets to the rug so they can review the goals they've set (see Share).

✔ Display the chart "Tools for Solving and Checking Hard Words" (see Share).

MINILESSON

CONNECTION

Explain how readers can be just like movie directors, using their imagination to turn the pictures and words in a book into a movie in their mind.

"How many of you love to watch movies?" Hands shot up instantly, as I had expected. "Me too! Well, did you know that it is someone's job to make those movies? I don't mean the actors, either. I'm talking about the directors. Movie directors read and read and read, just like you. And when they are reading, they are also doing lots of thinking. You see, they use their imagination to picture what's happening and actually start to *see* it in their mind, just like a movie.

"I'll bet all of you could do that job, too. You can be a director every time you read your books—using your imagination to turn the pictures and the words on the page into a movie in your mind. That way, you'll understand what's happening even better. How about it?" The children cheered.

❖ **Name the teaching point.**

"Today I want to teach you that another tool readers use to understand their books is their imagination. Readers pay attention to what's happening and imagine more than just what's in the pictures. They use their imagination to turn the pictures into a movie in their mind."

Add to the chart.

ANCHOR CHART

Tools for Understanding Our Books

- Check that you're getting it!
- **Make a movie to picture what's happening.**

Make a movie to picture what's happening.

TEACHING

Use the pictures and the words in the class demonstration text to imagine what's happening.

"So let's get to work. Let me use the pictures that are here and the words on the page to make a movie in my mind," I announced, placing the text under the document camera and flipping to page 20. "You all have such great imaginations, you can make this movie right along with me! Ready, directors?" I read aloud:

> Ivy sighed. She hugged Princess Mimi
>
> and added her to the box.
>
> Zelda buried the time capsule under the
>
> cherry tree.

I stopped to carefully examine the illustration. "Hmm, . . . I'm going to use the picture to help me make a movie in my mind. Well, in the picture, I see Ivy hugging Princess Mimi. She looks pretty sad. And Zelda is holding out the box with her nose in the air like she's waiting. But wait," I slid my finger back to the words, "the picture doesn't show *everything* that's happening. It doesn't show Ivy sighing or adding Princess Mimi to the box or Zelda digging the hole for the time capsule. I've got some work to do to make the movie in my mind show the *whole* scene. Okay, ready? Lights . . . camera . . . action!"

I closed my eyes, tapped my temple, and began to narrate how the movie might go. "I can see Ivy squeezing her Princess Mimi doll so, so, so tight because she doesn't want to let her go. Then I can hear her taking a big deep sigh." As I spoke I held an imaginary Princess Mimi and sighed deeply.

Then I opened my eyes and checked the picture for some more information. "Oh I see Zelda's foot is up. I'll bet she's tapping it, like she's impatient and waiting for Ivy to put Princess Mimi in the box. She even has her hand on her hip, like this," I motioned, exaggerating the movement and sticking my nose in the air. "Oooh, and in the next part of the

As students begin to read more complex texts, they'll need to do more envisioning. You'll want to help readers get good at doing this now, while they still have the support of some illustrations. It will serve them well in the future.

Ultimately, we want children to be able to imagine the story in the moment, as they read. However, synthesizing the text to bring it to life is a tough skill. Here we've slowed down the process to make it visible for the students.

movie Ivy gets up really slowly because she doesn't want to give up her doll. I can even imagine her giving Princess Mimi a little kiss before she puts her in the box."

"And cut!" I clapped my hands as if ending the scene with a director's slate. "Readers, did you just imagine all that was happening in this scene, just like a movie? I even saw some of you acting it out with me!" The class nodded eagerly. "I studied the pictures and the words to see what's happening in the story, and then I put all the details together to make a movie in my mind."

ACTIVE ENGAGEMENT

Read a few more pages of the text, prompting students to envision the next scene. Then have them turn and act out the "movie" with their partners, naming back all that is happening.

"Okay, directors. Ready to take over?" The children nodded eagerly. "While I read a few more pages, start rolling your cameras and picture what's happening in your mind like a movie. You might even act it out a bit, like I did."

FIG. 13–1   The class uses drama to help envision the next part of the book.

I set the book under the document camera and read a few more pages, pausing along the way and tapping my temple to indicate I was thinking hard to envision the scene. As I read on, many of the kids were acting out parts with simple gestures, playing pretend pianos as Ivy practiced on page 23. Others sat hunched over, their index fingers gently resting on their heads, or with closed eyes to picture what was happening.

"I can tell you're hard at work, using your imaginations to make a movie and picture everything that's happening in this scene. Turn to your partner right now and act it out together. Make a movie! And remember, say *everything* that you imagine, not just *what* is happening but *how* the characters are acting." I finished, making sure to leave the text and the pictures under the document camera as I moved around the rug to listen in.

Acting the story out as they read along can be a scaffold for readers who are just learning to do this work in their minds.

LINK

Review the strategies readers have learned to use to better understand their books.

"Readers, now you have two tools to help you understand your books; rereading when things feel confusing *and* imagining what's happening in the story to make a little movie in your mind." I gestured toward the chart. "Remember, if you're going to be the movie director of your books, it helps to check the picture *and* use the details in the words so you can imagine *everything* that is happening and understand your books even better. You can even act it out to show not just *what* is happening, but *how* as well! And if you're not sure, if you're not totally getting it, or your movie feels blurry, you can reread! Off you go!"

Strengthening Strategies to Support Comprehension

Follow up on the previous session's small-group work to support independence.

You might choose to start today's conferring work by following up with the higher-level readers you pulled together in the previous session. Decide if you'll continue to support the strategy you taught in the previous session or if you'll offer another tip for maintaining meaning in more complex texts. For example, if you choose to return to the work of attending to setting and time, you might quickly remind students of what you did together in the previous session and coach them not only to notice these changes, but also to *use* them to better envision the text. You might stop a child who is reading *Upstairs Mouse and Downstairs Mole*, by Wong Herbert Yee, to say "You are reading carefully! You noticed that it's evening as mole is walking to his mailbox. Can you use that information to imagine the scene? What might it look like? Maybe it's starting to get a little dark outside. Are you picturing what that would look like? And now that it's evening, at the end of a long day, are you imagining that he's probably walking slowly, thinking about *all* the things that have happened since morning? What might he be thinking about?" Then move to the next child, prompting in a way that strengthens and consolidates the previous session's learning.

Reflect on your teaching decisions to ensure that students are receiving instruction that balances problem solving words with reading for meaning.

As you make decisions about which students you will work with, look back over your notes to reflect on your teaching. Be aware of patterns in your teaching that could unintentionally be holding students back. For example, struggling readers often get more instruction on working with words in isolation. While this may come from the need to develop better decoding skills, these students also need teaching that supports their comprehension in continuous text. Guided reading gives you an excellent way to do this, allowing you to coach kids in problem solving at the word level, but within the greater context of reading a whole book for meaning.

In addition, you could pull together some of these readers for a strategy lesson with a focus on monitoring for meaning. Set the purpose for the group, perhaps teaching that one way readers help themselves understand their books better is to ask questions as they read. You might then use your demonstration text to read aloud a little, and then pause to model questions that support both literal comprehension and inferential thinking. For example, the question "How many objects are in the time capsule?" would lead children toward rereading to clarify events that are clearly spelled out in the text. On the other hand, the question "Why does Ivy take a deep breath before she tells Zelda the jewel is missing?" encourages inferential thinking and tentative ideas about the kind of characters Zelda and Ivy are. A child might respond by suggesting that maybe Ivy is worried that Zelda will get mad at her, because Zelda seems a little

(continues)

MID-WORKSHOP TEACHING   **Noticing Time and Place**

"Readers, put a thumb up if you've been really imagining the story and making a movie in your mind as you read!" A sea of thumbs appeared as I smiled at the group. "I knew it. I knew you all were great at using your imagination, and I'll bet it's really helping you to *understand* your books.

"Well, readers, as we make a movie in our minds, we have to make sure the movie is including *all* the parts of the story. We don't want to just imagine *who* is in the story and *what* they are doing. It's also important to imagine *where* they are and *when* they might be doing something. Authors often leave behind clues to help you imagine *where* and *when*. You can use the pictures, but you can also look out for words like *At home* . . . or *In the morning* . . . As you read, pay attention to clues that can help you understand *where* the characters are and *when* the story is happening, and then make sure your movie matches! Remember, if you're not getting it, reread!"

TRANSITION TO PARTNER TIME
Acting Out Scenes to Understand What's Happening

"Okay, directors, thumbs up if the movies in your mind are already helping you understand your books even better." Children signaled. "Today, when you meet with your partners, one way you can work together is to act out those movie scenes. You already know that when you're writing a story, acting out what people are saying and doing brings the story to life. You notice details you didn't think of the first time. And here's the cool thing: acting out the story not only helps you *write* books. It can also help you *read* books! You can pretend to be the characters, acting out *what* they are saying and doing and *how* they are saying and doing it. You can bring the movie in your mind to life. Especially when a book is feeling tricky, acting it out can help you understand details you didn't really get the first time."

I added this new strategy to the partner chart.

> **ANCHOR CHART**
>
> ### Reading Partners Work Together
>
> - We give reminders.
> - We grow ideas together.
> - We give book introductions.
> - We don't just tell—we HELP!
> - We do SOMETHING at the end.
> - We work together to solve hard problems.
> - We keep track of what's happening.
> - We think, "What might happen next?"
> - **We act it out to understand.**

We act it out to understand.

"Remember the special Post-it note I gave you yesterday to mark a tricky part in your book to talk about with your partner? Today you can also act those parts out to help you understand them better!"

bossy. Both questions support the development of stronger comprehension skills. After trying this out together, have students play a little game, selecting an independent reading book and, in partnerships, reading a page or two before stopping and taking turns to ask and discuss a question. As students read together, you can still interject with prompts for word solving, but the focus of this group will be on doing the thinking work that helps kids hold on to meaning as they read. Aim to have instruction that is well balanced for *every* child.

Staying on Top of Goals

Remind readers that they are always working on becoming better word solvers as they read.

"Readers, I saw so many of you acting out your stories today and talking more and more about your books. But now that we're building our new toolkit to help us understand our books better, we don't want to forget all the tools we learned for solving tricky words." I gestured to the "Tools for Solving and Checking Hard Words" chart that we'd built in the last bend and the new "Tools for Understanding Our Books" chart we just started. "Remember, you need to read the words right to make sure you've got your movie right!

"Let's quickly reread our word-solving chart to help us remember all the tools we have." I pointed to the Post-it notes on the chart, and the kids started reading without my help. "Great!" I announced. "Now get out your word-solving toolbox, the sheet where you each made a goal a few days ago. Read it right now, and share your goal with your partner." As students started to discuss their goals I voiced over some suggestions. "Tell your partner how this goal is working out for you," I said. "Are you getting better at using this tool? Do you need some help?"

I pulled the class back together to close the session. "Remember, readers, we only get better at something if we work on it, so don't forget to keep your goals in mind. You might even make a little plan to read your goal right before independent reading tomorrow so you can remember to use it more and more!"

FIG. 13–2   Alan proudly shares a spot in his book where he successfully practiced his goal.

Readers Keep Track of Who's Talking as They Read

MINILESSON

In your connection, you might tell a story about watching a movie with the sound turned way down. You might say, "My friend's newborn baby was fast asleep, so I turned the volume way down on the TV so the noise wouldn't wake him. Well, I could *see* everything that was happening and pay attention to the actions, but I couldn't *hear* anything anyone was saying, so I wasn't sure what was going on. I didn't understand the movie!" Connect this to the work readers have to do, paying attention to both the action and the dialogue to fully comprehend the story.

Then, name the teaching point. Say, "Today I want to teach you that to really understand your books, it's important not just to pay close attention to the *actions*, but also to pay attention to the *dialogue*. Readers keep track of who's talking as they read." Then, add that strategy to the class chart.

During your teaching, you'll want to demonstrate how readers can help themselves keep track of conversations in their books. For example, you may use page 25 of *Zelda and Ivy: The Runaways* to remind children to check the picture and make a movie in their mind to envision the scene clearly. You'll want to think aloud to help children transfer this work to their own reading. Say, "Who's in this scene? Oh yes, Zelda is there. She's coming out of the bushes. And Ivy is in the garden." Then, projecting the text with a document camera, show students how you use cues in the text such as quotation marks and dialogue tags to follow the speaker. "I see quotation marks here and here. That lets me know this part is dialogue. Who's talking? Oh wait, I see Zelda's name here. 'Out stepped Zelda.' Zelda must be talking here. And here I see more quotation marks. 'Just checking on Princess Mimi . . .' Is Zelda talking again? Oh no, here it says, 'Ivy admitted.' Now Ivy is talking." You might choose to model rereading the section of dialogue to support your comprehension of the text.

In the active engagement, you might choose to prompt partners to practice, using another page of your demonstration text. For example, you may turn to page 27 of *Zelda and Ivy* and coach students to use the picture, along with envisioning the text, to practice naming the characters in the scene. Then, use cues such as quotation marks, dialogue tags, and names to track the speaker.

Link this work to the tools students are using to build and fix up their understanding of their books. Remind readers always to check that they are "getting it" as they read, keeping track of what's happening and what's being said to understand the story, and stopping to reread when the movie in their mind is fuzzy.

CONFERRING AND SMALL-GROUP WORK

As you confer and pull small groups today, you'll want to support students in working toward their goals. Start a conference with a little research asking *where* and *how* the reader tried this work in her book. You could then have the child read on in her text, trying this work on the run. Selecting goals is very challenging for a first-grader! As you listen in you might realize that the reader would be better off working toward a different goal. First, honor the attempts the child made, complimenting her hard work toward getting better as a reader. Then suggest an alternative or additional goal. If the word-solving goal seems to be a good fit for the child, you might consider adding a goal around monitoring for meaning. You could use the chart for this third bend as a guide. Show the reader how to do this work, coach her in trying it out, and add the goal to the child's goal-setting sheet before moving on to the next student.

You might also want to check in with small groups you have worked with earlier in the unit. Pull a group together quickly and, using a new text, have them try out some of the work you previously taught. As students work, watch to see if they are able to use the strategy independently. Make sure to jump in to reinforce or reteach if necessary. Remember, applying new learning across different texts can be hard for children to do and may take time. Repetition and lots of encouragement will be essential.

Mid–Workshop Teaching

For your mid-workshop teaching, extend the work of today's lesson by pushing readers to think about not only *who* is saying what, but also *how* they are saying it. Teach children that the words in the book sometimes give clues about *how* the characters sound. Urge readers to think about how the character is feeling and to be on the lookout for words like *whispered*, *shouted*, *mumbled*, or *cried* to read in a way that matches how the character sounds.

Transition to Partner Time

When you transition to partner time, suggest a way that partners can continue to practice keeping track of the speaker. You might invite students to take on different roles in the story to read (and perform) dialogue,

requiring that readers attend to quotation marks and dialogue tags as they move through the text, reading aloud their assigned part.

SHARE

During today's share, you might orchestrate a small Reader's Theater with a few pages of a familiar text. You could use your demonstration text, with which children are becoming increasingly more familiar, or a shared reading text, such as *Tumbleweed Stew*. Assign small clusters of children a role to read, such as the narrator, Jack, Longhorn, Armadillo, and so on. Then, lead a shared reading to perform a few scenes, supporting students' ability to track who is speaking, as well as to consider *how* the character sounds.

FIG. 14–1   Partners dramatize their roles.

Readers Don't Just *Read* Words, They *Understand* Words

MINILESSON

CONNECTION

Remind students of the work they did as readers of nonfiction to understand new vocabulary.

"When you read nonfiction books, you know that there will be words you may have never even heard before, words that will teach you even more about a topic. You learned that readers can't just ignore these words—or mumble through them—because they help you get smarter about *the world*. Well, I have important news for you: you'll find words you've never heard before when you read *fiction* books, too. It's true!

"And you can't ignore new words when you read stories, either. You'll need to use your tools to figure out how to *read* the words. Then, you'll need to work hard to *understand* the words. These words will help you get smarter about *the story*, and understand what's happening even better."

❖ Name the teaching point.

"Today I want to teach you that readers learn new words from *all* the books they read! When you figure out how to *read* a word, but you don't know what it means, you stop and think about it. You can look for clues in the picture and the other words to *understand* the new word the best you can."

IN THIS SESSION, you'll remind children how to stop and use clues in the illustrations and the text to infer the meanings of unfamiliar vocabulary, extending what they learned to do with nonfiction books to all the books they read.

GETTING READY

✔ Clip the "Tools for Understanding Our Books" chart to the easel and have the new strategy Post-it note—"Say the word the best you can. Think about what it means."—ready to add (see Connection).

✔ Choose two challenging words in your demonstration text that you can use to model and give students practice with inferring the meaning of unfamiliar vocabulary. We use *concoction* on page 29 and *gazed* on page 32, both in Chapter 3 of *Zelda and Ivy: The Runaways* (see Teaching and Active Engagement).

Add the strategy to the chart.

ANCHOR CHART

Tools for Understanding Our Books

- Check that you're getting it! (Reread to UNDERSTAND it better.)
- Make a movie to picture what's happening.
- Keep track of who's talking.
- **Say the word the best you can. Think about what it means.**

Say the word the best you can. (gazed)

Think about what it means.

TEACHING

Admit the mistake of ignoring a new word, and then demonstrate the work of stopping to read and understand the word.

"I have to admit something to you," I looked at the class with a guilty glance. I began sheepishly, "I started reading the next chapter of *Zelda and Ivy*."

"Without us?" one child called out, in shock.

"I know! I was so excited to read more about these two, but that's not all. You see, there was a word that I had never heard before, and I just mumbled through it and kept reading. But I realized that I didn't really understand what was going on. I also felt that I didn't take charge of my reading because I just ignored the word. So, I'm wondering if you'll give me a second chance to be the boss and try again. Will you?" the children smiled and nodded. "Phew! Thanks! Okay, let me start over, and *this* time when I get to a brand-new word, I'm not going to ignore it. I'm going to work hard to *read* and *understand* the word."

You'll want to expand on the work readers learned to do to understand key words in non-fiction. As readers move up levels the vocabulary in their books becomes less controlled, so you'll need to teach children strategies to help them both notice and define unfamiliar words in all the texts.

I placed the book under the document camera and turned to page 29, the beginning of "Chapter 3: The Secret Concoction." I tapped under the word *concoction*. "This is the word. It was right in the title, so I kind of just mumbled through it. Let me drop that bad habit and work hard to *read* this word." I slid my finger across the word, using word parts to pronounce it. I did this quickly so that I could concentrate this lesson on the work of defining the word. "The Secret Con-coc-tion. Concoction? Well, I can *say* the word, but I still don't know what it means. I'm going to use the picture and the words on the page to help me understand it better."

I scanned the page, studying the illustrations. "I see this jar right below the title. There seems to be liquid inside. Oh, and here I see Ivy holding that same jar. Maybe the words will give me more clues." I began to read the first page of the chapter:

> Early one morning, Zelda sat down to write a haiku poem for her grandmother.

"Hmm, . . . I don't think that has anything to do with the concoction. I'll keep reading."

> Ivy came in, shaking a jar of liquid.

"Oh, that might be a clue. It's the jar. And yes, I was right, there's liquid inside it." I read on.

> "'What's that?' asked Zelda.
>
> "I'm making a secret concoction," said Ivy. She poured in some orange juice.

"Hmm, . . . she's pouring in orange juice. Maybe a concoction is like a drink. I'd better keep reading to see if there are more clues."

> "You should add glue," said Zelda.
>
> "I don't think so," said Ivy. She mixed in a mint leaf and an eyelash.

"Wait, now she's putting an eyelash in? Yuck! Maybe a concoction is some kind of weird mixture, or like a magical potion. Thumbs up if you're thinking the same thing." The class signaled with thumbs up.

While it may seem like you are now asking students to problem solve at the word level again, keep in mind that all of your teaching from the last few sessions will support this vocabulary work. In many cases, students can implicitly understand the meaning of new words if they have a strong understanding of the context. Rereading for clarification, envisioning, and navigating dialogue will all help to set students up for understanding the context of these new words.

Here, you show kids how to keep an open mind while figuring out the meaning of a word. Encourage readers to be tentative about this work, saying "Maybe it means . . . or maybe. . .". As they read on, students will then change or confirm their ideas. Like all of the problem-solving work in this unit, flexibility is key.

"So let me see if I can talk about this word to show that I understand it. A *concoction* is a kind of liquid, it's like a mixture of things, it's like a drink, but it's not really a yummy drink because there are a lot of things mixed up in it. It could be a like a magical potion.

"What do you think? Did I get the job done? Did I work hard not just to *read* the word but also to *understand* the word?" The kids nodded. "Terrific! Are you ready to take over, bosses?"

ACTIVE ENGAGEMENT

Read the next page of your demonstration text, asking children to signal when they notice a new word. Then, prompt partners to work together to solve it.

"If you hear a word that feels new, and you're not totally sure what it means, give me a *stop* signal so we can try *something* to *understand* the word." I turned to the next page and read aloud:

> Ivy screwed the top back on the jar. "No," she said.
>
> "What are you going to do with it?" asked Zelda.

I turned to look at the students. "So far so good? Let's keep reading. Stop me if you notice a new word that we need to work to understand." I read on:

> "We'll see," said Ivy. She gazed at the jar. She wasn't sure herself.

Several children held their hands up to give a stop signal. "I see some of you heard a word that you're not totally sure about." I placed the book under the document camera. "Is it *jar*?" I asked, wanting to provide a stark contrast between a familiar word and new vocabulary. The students shook their heads. "Is it *gazed*?" The students nodded. "Some of you may know this word, but let's all work together to talk about it. With your partner, use the picture and the words on the page to understand what this word means. Then, talk it out. You can say, 'It's like . . .' or 'It's not like . . .' to explain it the best you can."

It will be difficult to home in on a word that is authentically new vocabulary for every child, and that's okay. Even if some students know the word, they can still practice applying the strategy to define the word and articulate its meaning and, in the process, understand the word even better.

I left the page projected on the document camera and moved around the meeting area to listen in and coach partners to talk about the word. I prompted children with lean reminders like "Does the picture help?" "What's happening in this part?" "Read around the word." "What's another word that might fit there and make sense?" "What kind of word is this?" Then, I called students back together.

Talk about the word to help students articulate its meaning using synonyms, antonyms, and movement.

"Many of you noticed what Ivy was doing in the picture. Then, you read the words on the page and realized that *gazed* is something she's doing, something 'at the jar.' It seems like her arms are stretched out and she is looking at the jar. Maybe *gazed* is like *looked* or *stared*. Could those words fit in this sentence, too? I think *gazed* is like *stared*, but not quickly like this," I said, holding out my arms as if holding a jar and glancing quickly, then turning away. "I think *gazed* is like this," I said. I held out my arms again and stared quietly for a longer moment. "Will you gaze at something?"

Integrating movement, in this case acting out a word, can help children anchor memory around the word. Find opportunities to do this often, especially to build understanding of new vocabulary.

The kids all fixed their eyes on objects around the room. "I see Brandon gazing at the calendar. And Laura is gazing at the charts. Oh! Monica and Kira decided to gaze at the book bins. Will you gaze back at me now?" I waited for everyone's eyes. "Hmm, . . . so Ivy *gazed* at the jar. She must be thinking hard about that concoction. She's not sure what she'll do with it yet."

LINK

Recap today's strategy, reminding readers to stop and solve new words in both fiction and nonfiction books.

"So, readers, from now on, *whenever* you read and *whatever* you read, be sure to notice when there is a word that feels new, a word that maybe you've never seen or heard before. Then, use all of your tools to figure out how to *read* that word and say it the best you can. But don't stop there! Use clues in the picture and the words on the page to *understand* the word so that you can talk about what it means. That will help you understand what you're reading even better."

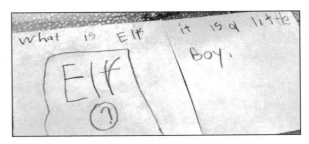

FIG. 15–1 Abdelrahman jots down a word and what he thinks it might mean, so that he can bring it to his partner to talk more about it.

Supporting Readers' Understanding of the Text

Support readers in developing their vocabulary through small-group shared reading.

You will want to dedicate some of your time today to supporting students in the challenging work of understanding new vocabulary. As students try this work in their books, they can sometimes become preoccupied with searching the picture and text for a clear definition. Instead, you will want to use your small-group work to offer additional guided practice to help kids understand that they can create an understanding of words through the process of talking about them. Before meeting with your students, plan for your small-group shared reading by selecting a text with a few new words to study. Keep in mind that you will typically want to work with words students are likely to use and see across a variety of contexts.

Pull your students together and start reading the text, letting the children know that when they come to a highlighted word, they will finish reading the sentence, saying

the word the best they can, and then stop to think about what that word means. Have the children first stop at a word you already expect them to know. Like much of the work in this unit, having students first try out a strategy on a known word helps them then to transfer the skill to an unknown word. Ask readers to look carefully for clues in the picture and text to help understand the word better. Then have them turn to their partners and explain what the word means. Encourage students to say as much as they can by giving them a small chart with prompts such as:

- Say what *kind* of word it is.

- Describe it.

MID-WORKSHOP TEACHING
Use Your Own Word to Replace New Words

"Readers, how many of you have already spotted a word in your books that feels new? A word that made you say, 'Huh? What's that mean?'" Hands went up across the room. "Marvelous! That means you're really taking charge, not just ignoring the word. Next comes an even bigger job—working to *understand* the word. You already know that you can use the clues in the picture and the words to help you figure out what it means. But here's another tip: you can also think, 'What other word might fit here and make sense?' Then, you can use your own word to replace the word in your book. That can sometimes help you understand what it probably means. Try this when you get to another new word in your books."

TRANSITION TO PARTNER TIME
Use New Words When You Book Talk

"It's time to meet with your partners, word solvers! And I don't just mean word solvers who work hard to *read* words. I mean word solvers who also work hard to *understand* words. Hands up if you figured out *one* new word in your books today. Hands on your head if you figured out *two* new words. Hands on your shoulders if you worked hard to understand *three* new words today! Oh my! Stand up tall if you figured out *more* than three new words." A few children stood up from their seats.

"Wow! Impressive! Well, your reading job isn't over just yet. You see, once you figure out what a word means, it's yours forever. That's right. You can use that word whenever you want, but especially when you talk about your book. So, push yourself to try that right now. *Use* your new words to talk about the story. Get started!"

- Think of another word that means the same thing.

- Say what it's *not*.

- Give an example.

For example, if you had students stop at the word *jogging*, they might say that it is an action word to tell how somebody is moving. They might say, "It's kind of like running, but slower. It's definitely not walking. It's faster than that. It's something people do for exercise, but a person doesn't *have* to be exercising to do it." In this way your students will be developing their schema for the word, using the words they have to fashion a greater sense of meaning around the new word.

After some practice on a couple known, or partially known, words, move to an unknown word. By now the process should feel familiar, and you will have created an environment where it is both safe and fun to speculate about the meaning of new vocabulary. You could then have students transition to trying this in their own texts, ensuring that they go back to their reading with a clear understanding that they can do this work with independence.

Support partnerships in helping each other monitor for meaning through drama.

Having reached the end of this third bend, you will also want to pull some small groups together to coach partners in helping each other use all they have learned about maintaining meaning with independence. You could pull two or three partnerships together and say, "Over the last few days, you have learned so many ways to help your partners not just *read* the words in their books, but also *understand* their books. Let's practice one of the ways we can do this." Then remind the group how partners can read a few pages of text and then act out the scene. Encourage them to make decisions about *how* to act it out or what to say by going back to the text to clarify misunderstandings, consider the meaning of new words, read passages of dialogue together, and discuss how they envisioned the scene.

Partners Can Teach Each Other New Words

Explain that partners can teach one another what new words mean as a way to build vocabulary.

"When I walked around the room today listening in to your book talk, I felt like I was in a *fifth*-grade classroom. You were using such impressive vocabulary to talk about your books. Sometimes, though, your partner will use a word that you don't quite understand. Just like you stop to work on new words in your books, you can stop your partner to ask him or her to explain the word and teach you what it means. That way, it can become your word, too. You can trade words like you trade bracelets or baseball cards! So, let's try it. Take out your book and think about a word you can teach your partner to use. You can explain the word, saying, 'It's like . . .' or 'It's not like . . .' You can even act it out to explain what it means, the way we acted out *gazed*. Partner 2s can start. Then, switch." As partners talked, I coached the children to talk about their words using comparisons and gestures.

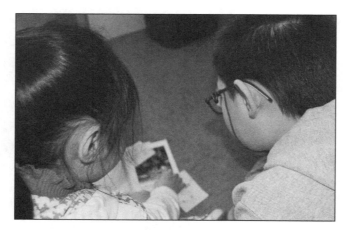

FIG. 15–2   Two students work together to trade new words and try to understand them better.

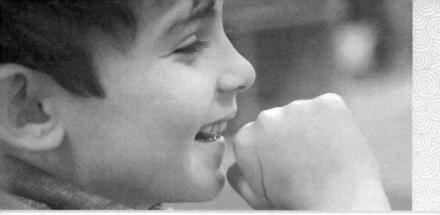

Readers Use Everything They Know to Get the Job Done *Quickly!*

IN THIS SESSION, you'll teach students to use everything they know, drawing from their full repertoire of word-solving strategies, to tackle challenges with greater automaticity.

GETTING READY

✔ Create a newspaper job posting looking for expert readers to record audiobooks for your school (see Connection).

✔ Choose a demonstration text that students are familiar with in which to model the work of the session. We use the first page in *Tumbleweed Stew*, by Susan Stevens Crummel, because children will know it from shared reading (see Teaching).

✔ Set students up to bring a familiar book from their book baggies to the rug (see Active Engagement).

✔ Make a plan for how students will create audio recordings across this bend. If available, use technology to set up a "recording studio," and post a sign-up sheet for it so students can work independently (see Conferring and Small-Group Work).

✔ Display the "Tools for Solving and Checking Hard Words" and "Tools for Understanding Our Books" charts for reference (see Mid-Workshop Teaching).

MINILESSON

CONNECTION

Share a newspaper job posting looking for expert readers to record audiobooks. Then, rally your class to take the job, launching the work of the final bend.

I ushered the class to gather in the meeting area in a hurry. "Quick! Quick! I have something important to tell you about!" The children made their way to their spots, and once they had settled, I held up a large page of newspaper ads. "When I read the morning paper today, I nearly choked on my blueberry muffin! You won't believe the advertisement I stumbled across." Then, vaguely pointing to one, I pretended to read a job posting:

> *WANTED: Kindergarten classrooms in desperate need of more audiobooks. The kindergartners have listened to every recording of a book in the whole school. Calling on expert readers who can make new audiobooks for the kindergarten listening centers. Help please!*

"When I first read this, I immediately thought of all of you and the reading you've been doing all month long. I thought, 'Hmm, . . . I wonder if maybe, just maybe, they'll be up for the job.' So, what do you say? Should we take the job?"

The children erupted in shouts of, "Yes!" and "Let's do it!"

"Wonderful. I'll make the call and let the kindergarten know that the first-grade reading bosses are up for the challenge. But it will be important that we don't just do this job to get it done, but to it really well. And to do that, you'll have to use everything you know—*all* of your tools—to make your reading the very best it can be!"

❖ Name the teaching point.

"Today I want to teach you that to be *really* in charge of your reading, you need to use everything you know, *quickly*! When you get stuck on a hard word, or on a hard part, use all of your tools to get the job done fast, and keep going."

TEACHING

Demonstrate a non-example as a way to help children distinguish between slow, staggered word solving and well-orchestrated reading.

"Okay, let me have a go at this work, too. Will you push the Record button when I start reading?" I pushed my finger through the air. "But be sure to hit Stop when I get stuck or slow down. I won't want to record any bumpy and boring reading. Ready? Here I go," I held up my copy of *Tumbleweed Stew* and then, clearing my throat, I began:

> *Jack Rabbit opened his eyes. He started [stretched] and . . . look– looked up at the pr [pretty] . . . um . . . pret . . . preet . . .*

"Wait, stop the tape, stop the tape. I need to figure this out." I held up my hand. "What can I do to solve this?" I looked up at the chart. "Well, let's see. I can think about what's happening in the story. I can look at all the parts of the word and read it part by part." I began listing strategies slowly across my fingers. "I can think about what *kind* of word this is to figure out a word that would make sense and sound right here. You know, I have *lots* of tools to fix this up. But wait! I'm keeping my listeners waiting with all this stopping and thinking. I need to use everything I know and get the job done *quickly*! Let me try again to stop and solve this faster. Okay, press Record!" I picked up the book and began again:

> *Jack Rabbit opened his eyes. He str- [glancing up at the picture] stretched and looked [sliding my finger under the word] up at the pr-pretty blue sky.*

"How was that? Better?" The class nodded. "Did you hear how much better my reading sounded when I used my tools quickly to fix up my reading on the spot? Whenever you get stuck, it's important to use everything you know to get the job done quickly and keep going! Are you game to try?" Students agreed enthusiastically. I turned the page of the familiar shared reading text.

Jack Rabbit opened his eyes. He stretched and looked up at the pretty blue sky.

You'll want to gesture in clear, yet subtle ways to show children that you are using strategies quickly to solve words. You might glance at the picture, point to word parts, or reread quickly. In more explicit word-solving lessons, you would think aloud to problem solve, but you'll want to make this work more streamlined to illustrate the automaticity of an orchestrated reading process.

You'll want to consider accessible technology when embarking on audiobook angle to the unit celebration. You may choose to borrow school iPads or other recording devices and set up a station in one or two corners of the classroom to allow children to make audio recordings across the remainder of this bend. You may, instead, revise this "job posting" and call for reading buddies to read aloud to the children.

The celebration in Session 18 suggests doing both by getting together with a kindergarten class. First, your students can show off their reading skills by reading to buddies. Then, at the end of the session, you'll present the class with the gift of new audiobooks. You'll want to make plans for this celebration now in order to help your students prepare.

ACTIVE ENGAGEMENT

Coach partners to take turns reading a page from a familiar text, prompting them to draw from their repertoire of strategies to word solve with greater automaticity.

"I should warn you: this isn't always easy to do. So let's practice together. Take turns reading. Partner 1, you can begin by reading this page." I pointed to the page on the left. "Then, Partner 2 can read the next page. As you read, if you get stuck, be sure to remember all the tools you have. Then, try something to solve it. Do it quickly and keep on reading! When I hit Record, start reading!" I held out my finger and motioned as if pushing a button. As the students began, I moved around the rug listening in and coaching children to orchestrate all they know to tackle trouble with more efficiency. I prompted leanly, when needed. "Check the ending." "Reread and get a running start." "What word would fit there?" I voiced over for Partner 2 to start reading the next page when Partner 1 had finished.

LINK

Remind children to draw from their full repertoire of strategies to strengthen their reading and prepare for the work of recording audiobooks.

"So if you are going to do this big job really well and make audiobooks for the kindergarten classes, it will be *extra* important to take charge of your reading. Use everything you know, *quickly*!" I gestured toward the class anchor charts. "When you get stuck on a hard word, or hard part, use *all* of your tools to get the job done *fast*, and keep going. After all, you can't keep your listeners waiting and waiting! This week, you'll each have a chance to record yourself reading one of the books from your reading baggie. Choose one you think the kindergartners will love to hear. You can keep reading all of the books in your baggie, but make sure the special book you pick gets *extra* practice! Off you go!"

FIG. 16–1 Jintao and Destiny take turns recording their reading.

Once readers have some problem-solving skills under control, send a clear message that this work should be efficient. The goal should be to fix up trouble and then get on with the fun of reading. You might use the analogy of riding a bike to explain this to kids in the habit of inching through their text. Once you know how to ride (even through the tough spots), you'll want to jump on and get going!

Keep in mind that children who are still learning to use the problem-solving strategies you've taught may not yet be able to do these things quickly. You can still share this expectation with the whole class, but plan conferences and small-group work to support these students. That said, make sure you know your students well and insist that anything they know how to do, is done efficiently.

Logistics and Supports for Orchestrating Reading

Set students up to start recording themselves reading.

A portion of your conferring time today will be spent on logistics as you set students up to record their reading. In many classrooms, children will already be familiar with using technology to record themselves. If not, you may want to consider showing your class how to do this outside of your reading workshop time, perhaps teaching students by recording a whole-class shared reading. To give all of your students time to record their readings, you may also want to think about allowing students to work on their recordings at other times in the day as well.

You might assign readers who are reading with accuracy and fluency to be the first to record, giving other children more time to prepare. You also could post a sign-up sheet for students to add their names to when they feel ready to record.

> MID-WORKSHOP TEACHING
> **Taking Inventory of All Your Reading Tools**
>
> "Readers, you have lots of tools to fix up words in your books, and reading the words, of course, helps you understand your books. But guess what! When you work hard to *understand* your books, it also helps you *read* and *fix up* words! You see, readers use *all* of their tools together—the tools for reading and checking words and the tools for understanding the story. When you put everything you know together, it helps you become an even more powerful reader, so you can fix problems fast.
>
> "So right now, look across the charts, 'Tools for Solving and Checking Hard Words' and 'Tools for Understanding Our Books,' and reread all the strategies you've learned. Almost as if you're digging through your toolboxes, take note of *all* the tools you have. That way, when you get stuck, you can use them together, and use them well."

Support the orchestration of reading in one-on-one conferences, providing immediate feedback.

Consider using the recording device as a tool in your conferences with individual children who need support for orchestrating their reading. First, have the child read a page or two of text as a way to research the reader. Decide on a teaching point that will move the child forward, perhaps teaching that reading should always sound like talking. Quickly demonstrate what that sounds like, and ask the reader to try it in his book, making the page "sound like talking." The beauty of this prompt is that it not only supports readers in reading more fluently, but it also implicitly encourages fast problem solving and meaningful phrasing.

(continues)

> TRANSITION TO PARTNER TIME
> **Partners Work Together to Get the Job Done Even Quicker**
>
> "Can I tell you a quick story? When I was little, I used to help my grandpa fix cars in his garage. He would lie underneath and, every now and then, stick his hand out and tell me the tool he needed. He'd say, 'Wrench.' And I'd hand him the wrench. Then, after a while he'd stick his hand out again and say, 'Pliers.' And I'd hand him the pliers. But sometimes, he'd scratch his head, not sure which tool to use. Well, guess what! *I'd* take a look and pass him a tool. I'd say, 'Try this!'
>
> "That story reminds me of the teamwork that happens, right here, during partner time. You see, when your partners are stuck, you can remind them of which tool to use. That way, when you read together, you can fix up problems even quicker. So whenever your partners get stuck, hand them the right tool to get the job done fast. You can point to the strategy on your chart and say, 'Try this!'"

Show the reader how to start the recording. After a page, stop the recording and play it back. Ask the child, "What do you think? Does it sound like talking? Do you want to leave it or make it even better?" Very rarely will readers turn down the opportunity to improve their reading in light of such rewarding and immediate feedback. After a few opportunities to improve the reading, send the child back to his reading spot to practice the strategy across his *whole book*.

Practice reading orchestration through small-group shared reading.

Pulling everything together quickly is not easy, and for some students, this instruction may cause anxiety. You'll want to be mindful of these students and support them in a small group by doing the work together. Select a shared reading text that's slightly above where students are reading independently. After a quick introduction, start reading together. You'll want to be very aware of your pacing and keep the reading moving along to help students internalize the feeling of putting it all together. Plan the words you will slow down to problem solve. As you come to these words, quickly suggest a tool and use it together. "Let's reread and think what makes sense" you might say. Then immediately reread. As you approach the word a second time you could put your finger on the text so you all read the first part, then the next, then put it together. You might interject a quick prompt to check such as "That sounds right to me. You agree?" Then keep on reading.

Then, too, you'll want to insert comments that encourage monitoring for meaning. "I can't believe he did that! Are you thinking about what he might do next?" Encourage students to comment as you read, chuckling at the silly parts or posing questions, together experiencing a text in its entirety, and orchestrating *all* the thinking a reader needs to do.

Conclude your small group by giving each student a copy of the text and having them read it independently, coaching as needed to support efficient, meaningful reading work.

Readers Triple-Check Their Reading *Quickly*

Remind children to check their reading.

I instructed the class to bring their book baggies back to the meeting area and settle in their spots. Once the students were ready, I put on a serious face. "Boys and girls, I have an important warning that you need to hear," I said with concern in my voice. "In fact, all readers need to hear this, so make sure you pass this on to every reader you know. Here it is: taking charge of your reading and getting the job done *quickly* doesn't mean reading *carelessly*. Readers need to make sure to always check their reading. You need to triple-check it to make sure it makes sense *and* sounds right *and* looks right. If not, you need to try something else and fix it up right away! Just like you work to solve it fast, you also need to check it fast.

"So right now, take out one of your books, and let's practice this with partners. Take turns. As you read, work together to solve problems quickly *and* triple-check your reading quickly. Ask, 'Does that make sense? Does that sound right? Does that look right?' If not, fix it up. Then, check, check, check and keep on going." I prompted partners to begin as I listened in, nudging children to check for accuracy, even when they had read words correctly. After a minute, I voiced over for partners to switch.

FIG. 16–2 Abel reminds his partner to check a word after realizing it doesn't quite look right.

Readers Investigate Ways to Make Their Reading Sound Great

IN THIS SESSION, you'll guide students in noticing and naming what makes an audiobook sound engaging for the listener and then apply these same strategies to improve their fluency.

GETTING READY

✔ Find an audiobook of a familiar story so that students can investigate what the reader does to make his or her voice engaging for the listener. We've chosen a reading of *Frog and Toad Are Friends*, by Arnold Lobel, because students will be familiar with the text from read-aloud. If you have trouble finding a recording to use, you can make your own. Just be sure to model fluent and expressive reading (see Teaching and Active Engagement).

✔ Label a blank piece of chart paper with the title "Ways to Sound Like a Reading STAR!" and have blank Post-it notes ready to record what students notice. Prepare one or two Post-its ahead of time. We use "Scoop up lots of words." and "Look for clues like dialogue tags." (see Teaching and Active Engagement).

Instead of a teaching point, this inquiry lesson poses a question that you will investigate together as a class. An inquiry lesson gives your students the opportunity to take ownership of their learning and discover for themselves strategies they could use in their reading. You might remind students that they've done this before when studying mentor texts in writing. Today, they are doing the same in reading.

MINILESSON

CONNECTION

Challenge your readers to see if they can investigate for themselves ways to make their reading sound great.

"Readers, I had a big problem after school yesterday. I was thinking about how you have all been working hard to use your tools to figure out problems fast. And then I thought, 'That's not enough! You *also* need to think about the sound of your reading!'"

"So, I was trying to figure out what I could teach you to help you do your job really well and make your reading sound *great*. Now, I've read a *lot* of books aloud before, but I've *never* made an audiobook. So I sat here thinking and thinking about who I could call to help you. I thought about all my friends. Nope. Not one of them is an audiobook reading star. I thought about my family. Nope. None of them either. I was stumped."

"Then as I was moving around the classroom, I started singing our reading boss song." I absent-mindedly started singing, "Be the boss of your reading, be the boss," before stopping abruptly. "And *that's* when it hit me!" I left a dramatic pause. "I realized, *you* don't need an expert to come in and teach you how to do this! *This* class can figure out how to do this job all on their own! So I ran to the kindergarten class as fast as I could and borrowed a real audiobook to help you with this job."

"Right now, let's listen really carefully to part of this recording and try to figure out how each one of you can become a reading *star*. Let's see if we can work together to investigate this question."

❖ **State the inquiry question.**

"How do readers make their reading sound really *great*? What does this reader do that I can try, too?"

TEACHING AND ACTIVE ENGAGEMENT

Use an audiobook to conduct a mini-inquiry into what makes reading sound great. Demonstrate noticing and naming techniques the reader uses in reading fluently.

I unfurled a piece of chart paper that was blank except for the title, "Ways to Sound Like a Reading STAR!" Then I attached it to the easel and turned back to the class. "I'm going to play a little bit of this audiobook for you to hear. It's from a book you already know well, *Frog and Toad Are Friends*, by Arnold Lobel.

"Listen carefully, and ask yourself the question, 'How do readers make their reading sound great?' I'll be thinking about this question as well. Let's work together to list all the ways we can think of on this chart. Then, we can try those things, too."

I placed a copy of the text under the document camera so children could follow along as they listened, and pressed the Play button. After a few lines, I paused the recording. "Hmm, . . ." I said to myself. "How do readers make their reading *sound* great? Well, one thing I noticed right away is that this definitely does *not* sound like choppy ninja robot reading." The class giggled. "You know what I mean." I moved my hands like a robot while reciting, "'Frog-ran-up-the-path.' What makes this reading sound *great* is the way the reader scooped up his words. Let's go back and listen to that again." I replayed the audio from the beginning. "Wow! He's scooping up a lot of words!" I voiced over, as I quickly added that strategy to our reading star chart:

Ways to Sound Like a Reading STAR!

* Scoop up lots of words

I let the audio play for a few more lines before stopping again. "I just heard *another* thing that makes this reading sound great! Thumbs up if you also noticed the way he made Frog's voice sound like shouting in that part? Do you think he did that because of these words right here?" I pointed to the dialogue tag "shouted Frog" in the text, and the kids confirmed. "Hmm, . . . is that another way to sound like a reading star?" The kids nodded. I added "Look for clues like dialogue tags" to the list. "Readers, we've only listened to a tiny part of this audiobook and we've already come up with two important ways to make your reading sound great."

Ways to Sound Like a Reading STAR!

* Scoop up lots of words
* **Look for clues like dialogue tags**

Give students a chance to listen to more of the audiobook, noticing and naming how the reading sounds.

"Now it's your turn to add even more ideas to our chart. I'm going to go back to the beginning and play this whole page. There are so many things to learn, so listen carefully, and each time you hear the reader do something that makes the reading sound great, hold out a finger to help you keep track of what you notice."

By selecting an audio version of your read-aloud, a text that children already know, you free them up to listen to how the reading sounds. However, you could most certainly use any audiobook you have on hand.

Here you start off the inquiry by modeling how to listen attentively and name the things you notice. Having these strategies already prepared on Post-its, or written (and covered) on a chart, will save you time during the lesson.

I played the recording of the first page, watching as students began holding out their fingers, then I paused the audio. "Go ahead, readers, turn and talk. What made that reading sound so great?" I listened in and nodded, helping students name their observations. "You're right. The voices were cool! The reader changed his voice to sound like characters talking!"

I turned to another partnership and listened in. "Yes, he did sound like he was getting a little mad. He used his voice to show us how the character was feeling." As I moved from group to group, I listened in for ideas I did not anticipate, jotting them down on a Post-it so they would be ready to add to the chart.

Debrief, summarizing what students noticed, and add these observations to the new chart.

"Readers, you did a fantastic job answering the question 'How do readers make their reading sound great?' I heard people say that readers can make their reading sound like talking, read some parts slow and some parts fast, and even add sound effects! I also heard people say that readers can use their voice to show *how* a character is feeling, and read in a loud clear voice the whole time! Let's put all of these ideas on our chart."

I quickly added these tips to the chart.

LINK

Remind readers of all that they know about taking charge of their reading, and send them off to work with independence.

"Readers, *you* know how to be the boss of your reading. You know how to keep on trying even when your reading feels tough. You know how to fix up hard words using all your tools. You know how to make sure you understand your books. And *now*, after the way you took charge today, you *also* know lots of ways to sound like a reading star! Thumbs up if you'll try as many of them as you can!" The class held up their thumbs. "Awesome! I can't wait to listen in to all the reading stars in this room! Off you go!"

While you will want to highlight and help students discover a few key things in this inquiry, be open to your students' observations, making space to discuss their ideas and record them on the chart.

You may decide to play more of the recording to guide students to notice a few things they have overlooked.

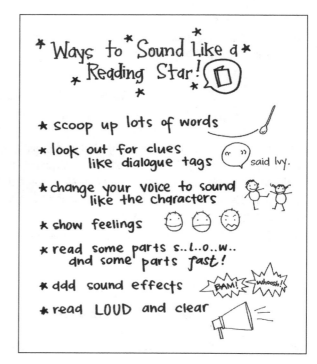

Teaching for Fluency and Reflecting on Data

Continue helping students with their audio recordings.

As students move into their independent reading, continue directing readers to the areas you have set up for their recording work. Today will be an especially fun day to do this work after all of your teaching on reading like a "star." Remember, these recordings will also be valuable evidence in your collection of assessments. Use them as a record of each child's reading fluency at this time of the year.

MID-WORKSHOP TEACHING
Punctuation Helps Make Your Reading Sound Right

"Readers, your reading is starting to sound *great*. In fact, I think it's starting to sound like a room full of audiobook reading stars! Before you continue, here's one more tip to help you make your reading sound *even* better. Don't forget that authors also give you clues about how to read your books, with punctuation. I know you already know to watch out for punctuation like periods and question marks at the end of a sentence, but pay attention, because that's not the only place you'll see punctuation. Authors also put marks like commas and quotation marks in the *middle* of sentences! You need to be on the lookout for these and use them to help make your reading sound better. When you come to a comma in the middle of a sentence, it means to take a little rest with your voice. And watch out for quotation marks. When you see them, make sure your voice is ready to sound like somebody talking!

"Will you take a minute right now to take a close look at the page you're on? Read that page right now, but be especially careful to look at *all* the punctuation, even the marks in the *middle* of a sentence. Use it to make your reading sound great. Try that right now."

Conduct quick conferences to assess fluency skills.

As you circulate among students, you'll want to pay attention to their ability to read fluently. Listen in as students read, considering:

- Pacing and the number of times students have read through their books

- The number of words a reader typically reads in each phrase

- Whether the reader uses expression to communicate an understanding of the text

- How closely the reading matches a student's oral language skills

- The extent to which a reader uses punctuation

(continues)

TRANSITION TO PARTNER TIME
Try Reading in Different Ways to See What Fits Best

"It's just about time for partner reading. As you read together today, remember to keep thinking about how your reading sounds. When readers are getting ready to read aloud, they sometimes have to try reading the text a few different ways. Your partner can help you do this. If you're not sure how to read a part, try it one way, then have your partner try it another way. For example, if you were reading the part where Frog shouts, 'Toad, Toad,' you might try it in a frustrated voice, and then in a loud, friendly voice. Remember to think about what's happening in the story, and use your imagination to help your reading fit. Listen carefully and, together with your partner, decide which way sounds the best."

- Efficiency in recognizing sight words quickly and solving unknown words on the run

Decide what to compliment and what to teach. One nice way to support the development of fluency is to read a text with a child, taking turns on alternating pages. Pinpoint an area to work on, perhaps using the chart from today's session for child-friendly language. Then take on the role of a proficient partner, modeling on every page you read and giving the child a chance to emulate that reading on the following page.

Use running records to assess the progress students have made over the course of this unit.

As you near the end of this bend, you will want to have evidence of student growth and begin to think ahead to the next unit. Use your time efficiently as you listen in on children reading today. Take a quick running record during this time and come back to analyze it later. Also make sure to record a few notes on how the reading sounded. As you look back on these records, you will want to look for evidence of the integration of meaning, structure, and visual information on every miscue.

Showing Off Your Reading Just Like a Reading Star!

Have students share the work they've done on making their reading sound just right.

I invited the class back to the meeting area and asked them to join another partnership, making a little group of four. "Readers, I asked you each to bring one book to the meeting area. After all your hard work making your reading sound great, I thought you might like to show off the way your reading sounds!"

I directed their attention to our chart for the day. "Remember, there are so many different things you can do to make your reading sound great. Let's read over our chart together to remind ourselves." We read through the chart quickly. "Now, take a look through the book you brought, and pick one page where you can make your reading sound great. Look it over and make a little plan in your head for how you are going to read it. Decide who is going to read first, and then share your reading, like a star!" I moved around the meeting area as each reader took a turn to read a page, giving compliments and joining in as groups applauded their enthusiastic readers.

As the reading dwindled down, I brought the session to a close. "Wow! I can't wait to see how much the kindergartners are going to love your reading tomorrow! They'll think their new audiobook is great. You are really thinking about making your reading sound the best it can be!"

FIG. 17–1   A "recording studio" for students to use during their independent reading

Partners Work Together to Make Their Reading Sound Its Very Best

We make our reading sound its very best!

Reread. Make it smoother!

MINILESSON

In your connection, you might prepare a short audio recording of yourself reading a familiar text with very little fluency. For example, you might read in a slow, staggered way or with little to no expression. You'll want to avoid overexaggeration. Instead, mimic the kind of discontinuous, inexpressive reading your children typically display. Then you might say to the class that you think you're ready to share your audiobook with the kindergartners. "Will you listen and let me know if my reading sounds its very best?" Elicit student responses, especially if children are hesitant to give critical feedback. Say, "Hmm, . . . that wasn't very smooth reading, was it? I'll need to try again to make my reading sound better. But how? What can I do?" Gather students' suggestions. Then, remark how helpful it is to have an audience to listen in and give helpful tips.

Then, name the teaching point. "Today I want to teach you that to make your reading sound its very best, it helps to have an audience. Partners can work together to listen in and give tips, like 'Reread this part again. Make it smoother.'" Then, add the new strategy Post-it note—"We make our reading sound its very best!"—to your class partner chart.

During your teaching, consider all the tips students suggested and then put them to use, rereading (and possibly recording a new audio file) to make your voice smoother and more expressive. You'll want to think aloud to link the shifts in your reading voice to the tips children gave (or should have given). For example, you might voice over, "Some of you said I should pay more attention to the punctuation. I bet that will make it sound more like talking when I read. Let me try that." You might even play a clip of the first recording side by side with the new recording to show the significant improvement, as well as the positive impact of feedback.

For your active engagement, coach partners to take turns reading aloud. Urge partners to listen carefully and give feedback, providing tips to help one another smooth out bumpy parts or add more expression, especially to lines of dialogue. You might voice over,

"Remember, helpful tips aren't helpful unless you try them. Reread, and do the things your partner is suggesting to make your reading sound its very best."

In your link, you might suggest that children begin their work time with partners before reading independently. This will give children two opportunities to practice this work in partnerships today, each time moving on to apply the feedback they were given as they read independently. For this first round of partner reading, you'll want to voice over after no more than ten minutes to shift kids into independent reading.

CONFERRING AND SMALL-GROUP WORK

As you confer and pull small groups, you'll want to take note of the progress children have made over the past several weeks. Look across your conference notes to check in with readers who have been working to be more flexible word solvers. Are they applying a larger repertoire of strategies to tackle words? Check in with readers who have been working to read in longer phrases and with greater prosody. Are they attentive to cues in the text, such as mid-sentence punctuation or dialogue tags?

Check in with readers who have been working to hold onto longer stories and retell with more key details. Research their ability to track the character and retell not only *what*, but also *why* and *how*, such as *how* the character's feelings changed from the beginning to the end of the story. It's especially important to note the current needs of your students at the end of a unit of study, as you'll want to carry these next steps into the next unit, helping students transfer the strategies taught when the content of your teaching shifts. This research will help you plan for conferences and small groups that will continue to help children grow as readers.

FIG. 18–1 Jintao and Destiny listen back to hear how the reading sounds.

Mid-Workshop Teaching

During your mid-workshop teaching, you might guide students to take out their mini-charts and check back, once again, with their goals. Say, "Check in with your goal—the tool you marked to push yourself to use more and think, 'Is this something I do all the time or is this a goal I'll keep working toward in the next unit?' Just because our unit is ending, it doesn't mean that your reading jobs are over. You'll have these tools forever! And you'll want to use them every time you read to get stronger and stronger and stronger!" Then, give students a chance to self-assess. You may even nudge children to set a new goal, carrying this tool into the next unit.

FIG. 18–2 After listening, Jintao and Destiny give each other feedback on how their reading sounds and come up with a plan to make it sound even better.

Transition to Partner Time

When you transition to partner time, remind the class that special visitors will arrive shortly and that readers will want to spend this time rehearsing for the reading work they'll do for their guests. Teach partners that to be helpful, they can give tips, but they can also give compliments. You might push children to make their compliments more specific by supplying language children can use. Say, "'Listen to your partner read and compliment parts that sound especially smooth!' You can say, 'I like the way you read that page because . . .' Then help your partner do that same smooth reading on the next page, too."

SHARE

During today's share, you'll celebrate the hard work your children have done across the unit. Invite a class of kindergarteners, or another neighboring class, as guests to give your students an audience for whom to read. You may also want to invite your school principal back to commemorate the end of the unit. You may decide to return, once more, to the class "Be a Reading Boss!" song and lead the class in a performance of all the verses, inviting your visitors to join in as well.

FIG. 18–3   Children share their reading with others.

Announce to the group that your students have been hard at work, using lots of tools to solve hard words and read tougher books. You might say, "The first-graders have been hard at work filling their toolboxes with lots of strategies for figuring out and checking hard words in their books. They've even added tools to read longer, tougher books! You see, the readers in this class aren't just readers, they are reading bosses! This means that whenever they get stuck, they take charge and use everything they know to get the job done. We are so excited to celebrate this hard work by reading to you! We even have special audiobooks to share with you so you can listen to these reading bosses anytime you'd like!" Then, partner your students with a visiting schoolmate or cluster students into small groups of readers and invite the class to read aloud to the guests.

You might close the celebration by sharing the audio recordings with the visiting classroom teacher or your principal. You might also tell your class that you'll make a special listening center so they can listen to their classmates' audiobooks! You could even choose to email these sound files to students' families or share them on a class blog! Whatever you decide, be sure to applaud the important strides your readers have made across this unit. Congratulations!

Read-Aloud and Shared Reading

Read-Aloud

Getting Ready: BOOK SELECTION

Across the read-aloud time for this unit, your goal will be to engage readers with early chapter books that support their ability to hold onto a story across multiple days. You'll want to be thoughtful about the length of the texts you choose to accommodate students' growing stamina, as well as their developing ability to follow a story thread. You might also consider supporting your transitional readers by reading episodic chapter books such as *Poppleton* or *Henry and Mudge* by Cynthia Rylant. In texts like these, each chapter works as an isolated episode, loosely connected to the other chapters.

We selected *Frog and Toad Are Friends*, by Arnold Lobel, because it is a part of a well-loved series about two endearing characters and their silly escapades and heartwarming friendship. Frog and Toad learn important lessons about friendship, and children are bound to relate to the ups and downs these characters face.

Be sure to choose a book that your students will enjoy; after all, engagement is everything! A powerful read-aloud will push kids to think deeply about books and to engage in conversations about characters (and topics) and will support their movement into more complex texts. You'll want to choose texts that reach toward end-of-year benchmarks (and perhaps beyond). You'll likely read texts at levels I/J/K or higher.

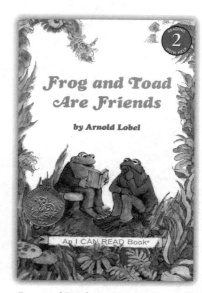

Frog and Toad Are Friends, by Arnold Lobel. Illustrated by Arnold Lobel.

Goals/Rationale/Prelude

- Many of your minilessons in this unit will focus on strengthening students' automaticity with print strategies so they can decode increasingly complex words. You'll also support students in self-monitoring and self-correcting at the point of error. Your primary focus in read-aloud is to improve students' comprehension and their ability to think more deeply about characters (or topics).

- As texts become increasingly more complex, the pictures become less supportive. You'll want to coach children to navigate this challenge across your read-aloud work. You might demonstrate how you stop to envision the scene, picturing where the scene is taking place, who is there, and what is happening. You might also move on to picture *how* the characters are behaving or speaking. Prompt students to envision, coaching them to check in, listening for details in the text to make their mind movies clearer. You might choose to ask children to quickly sketch a scene to hold onto the important details, or signal when their mind movie is going fuzzy to trigger a reread of the part, or page, to sharpen students' understanding.

- Throughout the sessions, you'll want to consider opportunities to support monitoring for meaning, pausing to accumulate the text or rereading to clarify understanding. You'll also engage children in noticing and solving unfamiliar vocabulary, coaching them to use the strategies you've taught to understand new words and to discuss their meaning with partners.

- You'll read the chapter book across multiple days, so you'll want to teach students the good habits readers have for holding onto longer texts. For example, you'll remind students to preview the text before the first read, and, at the start of each subsequent read, to recap what's happened so far. Then read on, support synthesis of the parts, and guide children to consider how the pages (and chapters) connect.

- As you come to the end of your chapter book read-aloud (and of each section or chapter along the way), it's important that you further support students' comprehension of the text and reinforce the habit of doing *something* at the end of a book. You might coach students to retell the big events of the chapter(s) together, helping them do this with more precision. Or you might lead a whole-group talk to share ideas and questions about the story, asking children to think about what they've learned about the characters so far and to make predictions about what else might happen. You might even reread a few pages and perform a scene or two from the book!

BEFORE YOU READ

Introduce the book and demonstrate taking a sneak peek of a chapter book, studying the cover and reading the blurb.

"Friends, I picked a book that I think some of you may know. It's called *Frog and Toad Are Friends*. Have some of you heard of these two characters? Wonderful! I thought that because you've all become such good friends in this classroom, we could read these stories and learn about *these* two friends. I bet they're a lot like you.

"Just like you do with your own books, let's start by taking a sneak peek at the cover and title." Hold up the cover or use a document camera to project it, giving students a moment to take in the details. "Just by peeking at the cover, we're already learning some things about *these* friends." You might elicit a few observations from the class. "Yes, they like to read and listen to each other! What thoughtful friends. Just like you! Let me flip to the back cover to check if there's a blurb that will give us a few more clues about these friends and this book. Oh, yes. Here it is. I'll read it to you. Will you think about the kind of stories we might hear in this book? Talk it over with your partner."

After students turn and talk, voice back a few responses. You might say, "Some of you said that maybe Toad will lose a button and Frog will help him find it. And some of you said maybe Frog will teach Toad how to swim. Do these things show how best friends are 'always there for each other' like it says right here? I think so, too! Let's read and learn things about *these* best friends."

AS YOU READ

After you've set up the class to read, you'll want to linger on the contents page to preview the chapters and anticipate what might happen in each episode or part. Show students how to connect the chapter titles to the details gleaned from the blurb on the back of the book. You might say, "Today, we'll read the first two chapters: 'Spring' and 'The Story.' The blurb on the back says that Frog and Toad are always there for each other. How might these two friends be there for each other in these two chapters? Turn and talk."

Pages 4–5: Recruit kids to use details from the blurb to think about how Frog might "be there" for Toad in this story. Then prompt a prediction.

As you read the first couple of pages, you will want to think aloud to consider what the characters are doing and why. This will help students monitor for meaning as well as pay attention to the details in the text. You might say, "What is Frog doing here? I think he's trying to remind Toad that it's spring. Why is he doing that? Maybe he's doing this because he's excited for springtime and wants Toad to be excited, too!"

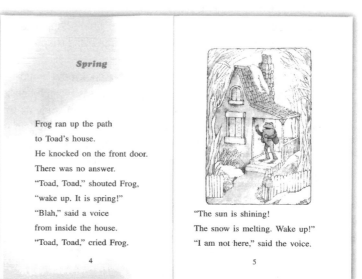

Spring

Frog ran up the path
to Toad's house.
He knocked on the front door.
There was no answer.
"Toad, Toad," shouted Frog,
"wake up. It is spring!"
"Blah," said a voice
from inside the house.
"Toad, Toad," cried Frog.

4

"The sun is shining!
The snow is melting. Wake up!"
"I am not here," said the voice.

5

118

Then ask students to turn and talk about what they are thinking. You might say, "The blurb on the back told us that these two friends are 'always there for each other.' How might this part show how Frog is there for Toad? What might happen in this chapter?"

Pages 6–7: Prompt students to consider what the characters are doing and why. Share a few responses.

As you read the next few pages you might want to release the scaffold, prompting students to consider what the characters are doing and why, without thinking aloud first. You might say, "What is Toad doing here, and why is he doing that?" After kids turn and talk, you could decide to share a few examples of things you heard partners say. Then, so as not to disrupt the flow of the story, continue reading.

Page 11: Stop and react to the story events, prompting children to share their own reactions.

Model how active readers stop to react to the text, responding to the story events. "Oh my goodness! Toad has been sleeping since November. He must be hibernating! We learned about that in one of our informational read-aloud books. But now its spring! (Turn back to the chapter title to connect the parts.) It's time for Toad to wake up. He's being very lazy. He won't get out of bed." Prompt students to share their own reactions with partners. You might voice over to get kids thinking more, "Think about what you might do if *you* were Frog."

Page 13: Pause dramatically after you read, "He came to the April page" and before you read the last line, "Frog tore off the April page too," to emphasize the decision Frog makes to trick his friend.

"But wait! It's still April! Frog is tricking Toad. But *why* is he doing that? Turn and tell your partner what ideas you're having about this." Listen in and share out a few responses. You might say, "I heard a few of you say that Frog was lonely without Toad so he had to find a way to get him out of bed. Some of you said that friends shouldn't trick each other and that Frog is lying to Toad. Let's read on and think about whether this was a good choice. Should Frog have let Toad stay in bed?" Finish the chapter and prompt children to share their ideas using details from the story.

Then, at the end of the story, you might have students think about this chapter. You might prompt children to think, "What happened in this story?" by asking partners to consider how "Spring" showed that friends are there for each other, linking, once again, to the details from your sneak peek. Or you might prompt children to consider how the characters changed across the story, saying, "Turn and talk to your partner about Toad. How did Toad change from the beginning to the end of this chapter?"

Read the next chapter, "The Story," prompting students in similar ways.

You'll want to do some similar prompting in the next chapter, scaffolding your students' thinking with listening prompts, turn-and-talks, think-alouds and gestures, such as a thumbs-up signal. You'll want students to think:

- What is the character doing and why?

- What might happen next and why?

- How does this part connect to the title/blurb?

SESSION 1: AS YOU READ

p. 11: Stop and react to the story events, prompting children to share their own reactions.

"Oh my goodness! I'm noticing that the character is _____. That makes me think _____. Think about what you might do if YOU were the character. Turn and talk."

- How did the character change?

- What happened in this story?

AFTER YOU READ

Review qualities of a strong book talk, recruiting the students to make a list.

Across the week, you'll probably recruit the class to reflect on the read-aloud in several different ways. You could, on this first day, engage the kids in a whole-class book talk that might go something like this: "We are going to have a book talk. You are becoming expert book talkers. What kinds of things do you do to have a *strong* book talk? Teach me!" You might choose to create a quick list as children offer suggestions, saying, for example, "These are wonderful things you should do *every* time you are talking about books." Or you might prompt students by referring to the "How to Have a Strong Book Talk" chart.

"Let's talk about these two chapters and do all *three* of these things. At the end we can reflect and check which ones we did a lot and which ones we need to remember to do more."

Engage the class in a conversation about Frog and Toad, perhaps discussing details that show that they are good friends.

"Our sneak peek told us that Frog and Toad are 'always there for each other.' Let's talk about what we learned from these two chapters about these best friends. Who would like to start our book talk?" Facilitate the conversation by coaching children to take turns speaking and adding on to one another's ideas. Encourage children to use examples from the book as they talk. You might distribute a few shareable copies to help students turn to specific pages across the first two chapters.

After your class book talk, lead the students in a self-assessment.

"Readers, will you think to yourselves: Did you, as a class, do *all* three things on this list? Let's read them together. Put a thumb up if you did this a lot, thumb sideways if you did it a *little*, and thumb down if you need to remember to do this more next time."

Read down the book talk chart and set a goal for the next read-aloud.

"Tomorrow, we will continue to read more chapters in this book. I can't wait to find out if the things we know about Frog and Toad as friends remain true or change!"

120

BEFORE YOU READ

Prompt students to list the details they learned about the characters in the first two chapters.

"Readers, today we will read the next two chapters in *Frog and Toad Are Friends*. But first let's warm up our minds to get ready to read. We took a sneak peek before we started the book, but when you're continuing to read the same book it helps to stop and retell what you know so far. Let's say what we remember about Frog and what we remember about Toad. Turn and tell your partner a list of things that we know about Toad. Say as many things as you can. Who is he? What does he do? What does he like and not like? How does he act?"

Listen in, and then call a few children to share their responses. "Now, talk about Frog. Go!" Share out a few things that were said to help children accumulate the details. "So, Toad is kind of lazy and he loves to sleep. Toad's best friend is Frog, and they like to do things together. Frog helps Toad *a lot*! Toad makes Frog laugh because he acts silly. He is hilarious. Frog, though, is not so funny.

"We really learned *a lot* about these characters in just two chapters. As we read on, I bet we'll learn even more. We might even get to add *new* things to these lists!

"Let's get ourselves ready to read the next story in this book. Let's reread the back cover again. Now let's read the title, 'A Lost Button.' Let's take a sneak peek at this *chapter*!"

Pages 28–31: Flip through the first few pages to help students get a sense of the story events, using the chapter title, the illustrations, and their knowledge of the characters.

"Using what you know about the characters, think about how the story of 'A Lost Button' might go. How will the best friends be there for each other in this chapter? Turn and talk." Listen in to assess the predictions children are making to consider if and how they are using their growing knowledge of the characters to make thoughtful predictions.

A Lost Button

Toad and Frog
went for a long walk.
They walked across
a large meadow.
They walked in the woods.
They walked along the river.
At last they went back home
to Toad's house.
"Oh, drat," said Toad.

28

"Not only do my feet hurt,
but I have lost
one of the buttons on my jacket."

29

AS YOU READ

Across the next few chapters, you'll want to work on helping your students learn more about the characters. You might coach them to think, "How do the characters feel and why?" and begin to describe the characters in more precise ways. Prompt students by asking, "What is the character saying or doing? How is he acting or behaving? How might the character feel?"

Pages 28–30: Think aloud to consider how the characters are feeling.

"I think Toad is feeling upset and a bit frustrated about losing his button." After the next page, you might ask students to turn and talk about Frog. After they talk, you could say, "I think Frog is acting like a good friend, a very kind friend, *because* he is willing to go back and help him look for it! That's what friends do when they are really there for you!" Find several places in this story to practice this skill.

Pages 33–34: Reread, thinking about *how* the character sounds.

"'That is not my button,' cried Toad. Hmm, . . . I think Toad is getting more and more frustrated. Let me think about *how* he's saying this and reread to sound like Toad." Reread the page, this time reading the dialogue with more expression to emphasize Toad's feelings.

On the next page, you might stop again and ask readers, "What does *wailed* mean? How do you think Toad is saying what he's saying?" This will help students think about the specific word choice used in the text, deepening their understanding and supporting vocabulary development. It also helps to reinforce rereading, to make sure your voice reflects the meaning of the words.

You might say, "Let me reread this part again, and will you think about what that word means with your partner? Turn and talk." Call students back after a moment to discuss its meaning. "Many of you said that you thought this part means that Toad cried or said it really loudly and upset. One of you suggested it might mean *mad*. You are right, in that it *is* a way that the character says something. Wailing is like crying—but crying really hard! So here's how I would have to read this part." Reread the text, emphasizing the meaning of the word. You might even choose to invite students to recite the line along with you, using expression to understand the word in context. Then you could find other places in the text where you want to prompt students to think about *how* something is said or *what* something means.

Page 37: Pause to discuss the meaning of a tricky phrase.

Stop and ask students to think about the meaning of phrases in the text, not just words. You might prompt, "What does this part mean? What does Toad mean when he says, 'What a lot of trouble I have made for Frog'? Let me reread this part and think about this sentence. Now turn and talk to your partners about what it might mean."

Read the next chapter, "A Swim," prompting students in similar ways.

In the next chapter, you'll want to do some similar work to practice thinking more deeply about the characters, considering what they are doing, how they are behaving, and how they might be feeling. You might also find places to discuss the meaning of words or phrases, prompting with questions like the following:

- What is the character doing and why?
- How is the character saying this? Let's sound like the character.
- How do you think the character is feeling now? Why?

122

- What might this word/phrase mean?

- How did the character change?

AFTER YOU READ

Remind kids to do *something* after they finish a book, and model one or two ways to linger with a book after reading.

At the end of the chapter, you will want to remind students that readers do *something* to stay with the story a while longer. You can give them a few options. Suggest that they retell the story, name a part to reread, or think about important things that happened in the story that they can talk about.

You may decide to give kids a brief summary of what happened in the chapters thus far or name a few important details you've learned about the characters. For example, you might say, "Not only is Frog the kind of friend who helps Toad when he has trouble; *but* Toad is also helpful and kind to Frog. They both are really thoughtful and helpful." You could then go on to say, "Let's name a couple of our favorite parts in this story to reread and talk more about! Rereading will help us think about more things we can say about Frog and Toad."

Remind readers to check in with their goals, pushing themselves to be active listeners during the book talk.

"Let's look at our "How to Have a STRONG Book Talk" chart to remember the three things you should do *every* time you are talking about books.

"Now, let's push ourselves to *add* on to what someone says. That's a goal we set for our book talk. Remember, you can say, 'I *also* think . . .' to keep the talk going."

Help students put the parts together to grow ideas about the character. You might stir some debate.

"Let's think about all the chapters we've read so far and go back to the title of the book and the blurb on the back. So the title is *Frog and Toad Are Friends*. And the blurb let us know that these two friends are 'always there for each other.' What details from the book prove this? Do you agree? Is this always true? Is Frog *always* there for Toad? Is Toad *always* there for Frog? Who would like to start the conversation?" Coach students to build on one another's arguments, providing more examples to support one side or the other.

SESSION 2: AFTER YOU READ

p. 52: Remind children to do something after they finish a book. Model a few ways to linger with a story after reading.

"Readers do something to stay with a story a while longer. You can retell the story, name some parts to reread, or think about the important things that happened in the story that you can talk about."

BEFORE YOU READ

Set students up to listen to the final chapter with a lens.

You might say, "Think about all the ways Frog and Toad are there for each other. And as we read the last chapter of this book, listen for more examples that prove that they are best friends." Or you might nudge children to consider the lesson this book aims to teach. "As I read, think about what important lesson you think Arnold Lobel wants us to learn about friendship."

AS YOU READ

Prompt readers to pay attention to what the characters are doing, how they are feeling, and why.

Pages 54–55: Prompt children to consider what the characters might be thinking.

"Toad is sad that he has never received a letter in the mail. What do you think he might be thinking to himself?" Voice back several possibilities to support students' willingness to take risks, especially when there is no one right answer. "I heard some of you say that Toad might be thinking, 'I wish someone would send me a letter.' Or maybe he's thinking, 'I never get any mail.' Or maybe, 'I don't like waiting for the mail.'"

Prompt students to do this same work to infer Frog's inner thoughts, coaching them to use what they know about Frog from earlier chapters. "What do you think Frog might be thinking? Use what you know about Frog." Listen in to assess whether students are drawing from patterns across the book. "We know that Frog is thoughtful and helpful. When Toad is upset, Frog finds a way to help him. I think Frog will find a way to cheer up Toad. Maybe Frog will write Toad a letter! I can tell that many of you agree! Let's read and find out."

"Yes," said Toad.

"This is my sad time of day.

It is the time

when I wait for the mail to come.

It always makes me very unhappy."

"Why is that?" asked Frog.

"Because I never get any mail,"

said Toad.

54

"Not ever?" asked Frog.

"No, never," said Toad.

"No one has ever sent me a letter.

Every day my mailbox is empty.

That is why waiting for the mail

is a sad time for me."

Frog and Toad sat on the porch,

feeling sad together.

55

AFTER YOU READ

Spark a whole-class discussion about the story's message.

"Let's think about not just this final chapter, but the *whole* book and all the things these two friends have done together. What important lesson do you think Arnold Lobel wants us to learn about friendship?" Call on one child to initiate the discussion. Encourage children to use pages from the book to support their ideas.

Use interactive writing to create a bumper sticker for the story.

"It sounds like *Frog and Toad Are Friends* is sending an especially important message for us because each one of you is a friend to someone. We'll want to make sure to hold onto the lesson from this book. Let's work together to make a bumper sticker for *Frog and Toad Are Friends* and add it to our wall. What might it say? What does Arnold Lobel want us to remember about friendship? Plan it out. Go!"

Listen in, collecting possibilities for a bumper sticker or two. Then call students back, deciding which parts of the word, or sentence, you'll ask them to help you record.

"I heard a few great ideas for a bumper sticker we can make. Maybe we can write, 'Friends are always there for each other.' Let's write that together. I'll need your help." Remember, you'll want to record whatever is currently too hard and whatever is too easy for writers. For example, you might ask students to come up to record word parts using familiar patterns or known words, such as using the word *day* to record *ways* in *always*. You might also ask a child to record the vowel team in *each* or the letters that make /er/ at the end of *other*. Add the bumper sticker to any others you've collected across the year. You might even go on to make a second bumper sticker.

SESSION 3: AFTER YOU READ

p. 64: Use interactive writing to create a bumper sticker for the story.

"It sounds like the author is sending an important message that we won't want to forget. Let's make a bumper sticker for this book and add it to our wall. What might our sticker say? What does the author want us to remember? Plan it out. Then we'll write it together."

Shared Reading

Text Selections

> *Tumbleweed Stew*, by Susan Stevens Crummel, Green Light Readers, Level 2

> Song of your choice, for example, "Be a Reading Boss!"

We chose *Tumbleweed Stew* because of the delightful characters, rhythmic text, and familiar storyline (a twist on the classic *Stone Soup* plot). The story contains a variety of action words for your students to learn and talk about, as well as rhythmic cadence and dialogue to allow for fluency and phrasing practice.

You'll notice that we chose a text that is above the benchmark text level for this time of year. This gives readers an opportunity to work on word solving, comprehension, and fluency in a more complex text with support and guidance.

DAY ONE: Warm-up, Book Introduction, and MSV

On this day, you'll introduce a song and book because you'll continue to reinforce the habits you've been teaching all year, such as starting with a sneak peek, studying pictures, rereading with a smooth voice, and thinking about the text. You'll also highlight the big work of this unit: developing the mind-set and the habits needed to solve tough words and continuing to read to understand more.

And so, in this first read, you'll remind readers of your first teaching point in this unit—that when readers are the boss of their reading, they can *stop* at the first sign of trouble and try *something* to solve the problem, saying to themselves, "I can do it!" Then they try lots of different strategies to tackle the tricky word. You might say, "Readers, I've been so impressed with how all of you have been taking charge of your reading by stopping when you notice a problem and then trying lots of different strategies to tackle those tricky words. Today I have a new book for you to take charge of. Are you ready?"

To support this work you'll want to make sure you have the "Be the Boss of Your Reading!" chart from Bend I prominently displayed so you can coach students to stop and try something when they encounter tricky words. You'll also want to display your growing word-solving chart so students can draw on their expanding repertoire of strategies.

Of course, reading is always about meaning, so on this first read be sure to leave space for comprehension, retelling the story with key details, and talking about new words.

WARM UP: "Be a Reading Boss!"

Quickly reread a familiar text (a poem, song, chant, or chart) to build confidence, excitement, and fluency.

You might begin your warm up with the "Be a Reading Boss!" song to create excitement for the job of tackling tricky words. You may not want to sing the whole song yet, depending on how far you have progressed through the first bend (your students learn one new verse each day).

If you think something's wrong, you've got to STOP! (clap, clap!)

If you think something's wrong, you've got to STOP! (clap, clap!)

If you think something's wrong, and you say, "What's going on?!"

If you think something's wrong, you've got to STOP! (clap, clap!)

Then you try something else, and don't give up!

Then you try something else, and don't give up!

Then you try and you try, and you say, "This job is mine!"

DAY ONE FOCUS

✔ Rally your students to be the boss of their reading, building on the goal of the unit.

✔ Coach students through the process of efficiently trying multiple strategies and drawing on all three cueing systems (meaning, structure, and visual [MSV]) to solve unknown words.

✔ Remind students of the word-solving skills they've been learning all year, and provide practice with the new skills they are building in this unit.

Then you try something else, and don't give up!

When you think you've got it right, check it out!

When you think you've got it right, check it out!

When you think you've got it right, triple-check with all your might . . .

> *Does it make sense?*
>
> *Does it sound right?*
>
> *Does it look right?*

When you think you've got it right, check it out!

Be the boss of your reading, be the boss!

Be the boss of your reading, be the boss!

When the job gets really tough,

And you want to huff and puff (cross arms and sigh)

Be the boss of your reading, be the boss!

You might end this quick warm up by saying "Wow, readers, what great singing! As we read our book together and find some tough words to tackle, I can tell you'll know just what to do!"

BOOK INTRODUCTION AND FIRST READING: *Tumbleweed Stew*, by Susan Stevens Crummel

Give a book introduction to provide the gist of the story and entice readers.

If your class is familiar with the classic story *Stone Soup*, you might point out that this week's shared reading book is another version of the same basic story. In the classic version, an old man makes stone soup for the villagers, and in this version, a jackrabbit makes tumbleweed stew for the animals on a ranch. Either way, you can begin by asking, "Have any of you ever heard of tumbleweed stew? Let's take a sneak peak and see if we can use the clues on the cover, the back, *and* what we already know to help us think about what it could be."

Then you might model thinking aloud as you peruse the cover, read the blurb and, if appropriate for your class, recall what you already know about *Stone Soup*. You might then prompt partners to turn and talk about what tumbleweed stew might be and to predict how the story might go. "Let's read to find out what happens when Jack tries to make tumbleweed stew for the animals." You'll want to keep your book introduction tight, leaving most of your time for reading the book together.

Before reading, you'll want to choose four to five words to mask for word-solving practice. Rely on data to make these decisions, thinking about what strategies and cueing systems students tend to use and which ones they forget about. Then carefully choose words in the text so students can practice these strategies. You'll want to be sure to spread masked words out across the text so that you can still maintain meaning as you read along together and students don't get the feeling that reading is only about solving words.

Read the text with fluency and expression, inviting students to chime in from the beginning.

On the first read you'll lead the charge, modeling expression and fluency for students as they chime in alongside you. You'll no longer want to point word by word because it will only promote choppy reading; instead, point to the beginning of each line to help students track the text as you read. Read the first few pages straight through, enjoying the beginning of the story together!

Stop at each of the words that you masked in advance, coaching students to stop, try something, try something else, and check it!

As you guide students into higher levels of text you'll need to be strategic about how you reveal visual information. Often you'll only mask parts of words, leaving the first few letters uncovered so that children immediately have this information. If the word begins with a digraph or blend (i.e., *shed*, *drop*) you'll leave both letters open because you want students to see these as individual units instead of two separate letters. Furthermore, if you've covered a multisyllabic word, you might layer Post-it notes so you can reveal the word part by part. As you peel away Post-it notes to reveal each part, begin to say them together while reminding students to think about what word would make sense. After you make your way through the word you will, of course, prompt students to check that it makes sense, sounds right, and looks right.

> Jack's tummy growled. He thought,
> *The sun is up. The sky is blue!*
> *What a great day for tumbleweed stew!*
> He hopped along, jumping over brush
> and cactus.

For example on the second page, you might cover up a word, such as *growled*, leaving only the first two letters, *gr*, visible. As you approach this word in the text you might say, "Oh, no, readers, what should we do?" Then you can reference the "Be the Boss of Your Reading!" chart so children can remind you to stop and try something. You might respond, "What could we try to solve this hard word?" gesturing at the word-solving chart and inviting kids to chime in with ideas. Choose one suggestion from the crowd, and guide students through the process of trying it out. You might say, "I heard some of you say we could reread and think what would make sense. Let's try that together. 'Jack's tummy gr-.'" Allow the children to chime in with what the word could be, "I heard some of you saying *grumbled*. That would make sense and the *beginning* looks right. Now let's make sure the *whole* word looks right." Reveal the word, sliding your finger under it and then perhaps breaking it part by part to figure out the word *growled*. You'll want to be responsive to your students in the moment, building on the suggestions they offer.

Invite students to think about the text.

Although you've got lots of work to do on this first day, you'll want to make sure comprehending the story doesn't get lost in the mix. As you read along you'll think aloud for the students. Early on in the text, when Armadillo offers up his carrots, you might say, "Hmm, . . . wait a minute! Armadillo was really rude on that last page, but now he's willing to add his carrots to the stew. I'm wondering why that's happening." You won't take the time to call on children, but by thinking aloud you'll encourage them to notice and think at these spots, too. You might also choose one, or perhaps two, places in the story for children to turn and talk. After Jack stuffs the tumbleweed into the pot you might pause and comment, "Oh, boy, readers, I'm wondering what's going to happen next. Turn and talk to your partner and make a prediction!"

AFTER READING

Like all readers, you'll want to do *something* at the end of the book.

When you finish reading you'll want to make sure you shift the focus back toward meaning, giving students a moment to sit with and think about the text. You might say, "What a great story about making tumbleweed stew. Let's take a moment to remember and retell the big things that happened in the story. You might even have some new ideas about what tumbleweed stew is. Turn and talk to your partner!"

DAY TWO: Cross-Checking Sources of Information (MSV)

Today you'll continue to focus on helping students use all three cueing systems. Even though students typically won't have much word-solving work to do on this second read, there certainly will be times when they'll make mistakes or feel uncertain. When that happens, you'll shift your focus from *solving* hard words to *checking* hard words.

You'll want to reinforce the idea of cross-checking sources of information as a good reading habit; when they're not sure about a word or when something doesn't make sense, sound right, or look right, readers stop and check it! On this second day, then, you won't need to cover words. Instead, as you read, you'll choose a few places in the text to stop and think aloud, perhaps saying, "Wait, did that make sense? Readers, I'm not sure. We'll have to check it!" You'll need to model checking your reading both when you've made an error and also when you've solved the word correctly but aren't sure you've gotten it right. Students need to understand that readers check until they're certain.

Again, you'll want to have your most current word-solving chart and "Be the Boss of Your Reading!" chart available to refer to, so that you can model using these tools as you read. You'll also support children to develop more fluency on this second read of the text.

DAY TWO FOCUS

- ✔ Orchestrate multiple sources of information to solve unknown words.
- ✔ Check to see that the reading makes sense, sounds right, and looks right.
- ✔ Practice using word-solving and word-checking strategies.
- ✔ Read for comprehension.
- ✔ Develop more fluency.

WARM UP: "Be a Reading Boss!"

Sing the "Be a Reading Boss!" song with your students a second time. Incorporate hand gestures and facial expressions.

You might begin by having students sing the "Be a Reading Boss!" song again to warm up for reading. You could say, "This song can help us remember all the smart things readers do when they get to tough words. As we sing, let's think of some motions we can do with our hands to make the song more fun. Let's think what we could do for the first line, 'If you think something's wrong, you've got to stop!'" As you continue through the song, engage students in inventing hand signals or gestures for the rest of the words. Also, you might ask kids to use their facial expressions to express different meanings in the different parts of the song.

Then you might accompany this with a quick rereading of your word-solving chart to remind students of the strategies they can use to help when the words get tricky.

SECOND READING: *Tumbleweed Stew*

Remind readers to continue using all they know to solve words and to check that they are reading with accuracy.

After singing the song, you'll want to compliment children on all the word-solving work they did yesterday and let them know that their work isn't finished yet. Emphasize that even when readers reread books, they can struggle with tricky words. One of the most important jobs readers have is to make sure they check that words make sense, sound right, and look right.

Buzzard floated down to take a look. "I can smell this food way up in the sky! It needs onions," he said. "I'll fly home and get some."

You'll want to choose a few words ahead of time that you'll coach children to check. There are a few ways you can set this up. You might decide to use highlighter tape or Wikki Stix around or under the words—to signal that they need to be checked. Or you could mask each word with a label or Post-it note on which you've written either the correct word or a partially correct attempt. When you reach each word in the text, you'll prompt students to check if it makes sense and sounds right before revealing the covered word to check that it also looks right. Occasionally you'll want to insert the correct word to emphasize that when readers check words, they sometimes find that they are already right.

Another method for helping children check is to let your voice trail off in key spots of the text. If you've arrived at a tricky part, you're likely to hear the group begin to mumble or try out several words. This is a perfect spot to stop and say, "Readers, it sounds like we have some different ideas about what this word could be. We'd better check it!"

Finally, you might simply pause the students as you read, modeling your own uncertainty. For example, when Buzzard arrives you might read, "Buzzard floated," and then exclaim, "Wait a minute readers, *Buzzard floated*? Does that make sense? We'd better check it!" Then guide students to triple-check that yes, it does make sense, sound right, and look right!

As always, be aware of your pacing, making sure that you don't stop to check so many words that the story is lost. We want to model reading a "just-right book," one in which children have work to do but not so much that they are constantly stopping and losing meaning.

AFTER READING

After the second read, give students an opportunity to talk more about the story by asking a few inferential questions.

"Now that we've read this book a second time, let's see if we can grow some new ideas together. Was anybody wondering a little bit about Jack? It seemed like he was tricking the other animals in the book. I'm wondering why he was doing that. Was he trying to be helpful or mean? Turn and talk to your partner. What do you think about Jack? You could start by saying 'I think . . .'" Here you might reference your "How to Have a Strong Book Talk" chart from read aloud to help students get started with this conversation.

As with most books, *Tumbleweed Stew* affords plenty of other opportunities to think deeply about the text. You could also spend some time thinking about the final phrases in the book, "Another day for being sly / What a great day for cactus pie." Coach students to unpack what these phrases mean in the context of the book. You'll want to angle any conversations you set up toward the needs of your students, so think about what kind of inferential work they need to practice and plan accordingly.

DAY THREE: Word Study

You'll use the same text as the day before, this time focusing on word study concepts, perhaps hunting for spelling principles you're working on with students. Again, you'll choose activities relevant to the word work students need. Lean heavily on your data, namely, word identification assessments, spelling inventories, writing samples, and running records. A critical skill for children as they move up levels is the ability to break words in different ways. Today you might take the opportunity to have children explore this skill with several known words in your shared reading text. Invite them to bring dry erase boards to the rug so that they can work with a partner to try this out.

DAY THREE FOCUS

✔ Build a sight word vocabulary.

✔ Study phonics.

✔ Grow new vocabulary.

✔ Connect what we know about words to our reading.

✔ Reread texts with more word automaticity and fluency.

WARM UP: Spelling Pattern Game

Quickly play a word study game with a focus on what students are practicing.

Today you might want to warm up by playing a fast word study game that prepares students to search for familiar word parts. For example, you might have children write on their dry erase boards a known word that contains a pattern they are studying. For example, "Readers, can you all jot the word *make* on your boards?" As children write, you'll prompt

132

them to write another word that connects to the word *make* by saying, "Great, now see if you can magically turn *make* into *shake*. What letters would stay the same? Which ones would change?" You might continue this game for several rounds, changing not only the ending of the word, but also the beginning, saying, for example, "Okay, now turn *shake* into *ship*!" Making connections between word parts will help students begin to see words in flexible ways.

Alternatively, you might decide to do a quick word sort, posting two spelling patterns in your pocket chart and then reading words aloud and asking students to identify the patterns they hear. You might say, "I'm going to read a word. See what spelling pattern you hear, /ake/ or /at/." As you read the word aloud, have children put a thumb on their knee if they hear /ake/ or a thumb on their shoulder if they hear /at/. Make sure to keep this game quick so you can get to reading the text.

THIRD READING: *Tumbleweed Stew*

As you read the text pause to break multisyllabic words in different ways.

As students move into these higher-level texts, the ability to fluently and flexibly break words in several ways is critical, and you'll want to provide plenty of opportunities for them to practice this work. Prior to reading the text, you might choose several words in the story to break in multiple ways, beginning with easier words. For example, when Jack meets Longhorn you might stop at the word *munching* and say, "Readers, let's see if we can think of a few ways we might break this work into parts." Then you could use magnetic letters to coach the children to see a few different possibilities. You'll slide the letters apart to emphasize the different options (m/un/ch/ing, mun/ch/ing, munch/ing, and so on). As you read farther into the text you might decide to set partners up to do this work with one or two words by writing them on their dry erase boards. The last two pages provide a range of opportunities for this work. Some children might choose more familiar words such as *opened* or *looked*, while others might tackle more difficult words such as *scamper*. You might say, "Readers, now you and your partner can try to do this work. Choose a word on this page that you'd like to work with and write it on your dry erase board. Then think, 'How could we break this work into parts?' There are so many ways to do this. I know you'll find more than one!"

Rattlesnake slithered over with some celery. "You can't make stew without celery," he said.

AFTER READING

Study unfamiliar vocabulary, using context clues and dramatization to determine meaning.

Building on the work of the last unit, you'll want students to develop an understanding of some of the key words in the book. *Tumbleweed Stew* lends itself to studying action words, and you might set children up to talk about and act out these words.

"Readers, I noticed in this book that the author used some really interesting words to describe how the animals moved. She didn't just say, 'They walked.' Instead, she chose specific, fancy words. Let's see if we can say as much as we can about them so we'll know these words really well, too. Maybe we can even use them in our writing."

For example, you could look back to the page when Rattlesnake arrives, carefully reading the sentence "Rattlesnake slithered over with some celery," and prompting students to act out *how* Rattlesnake arrived and then to say more about the word *slithered*. "Readers, let's talk more about this word. Turn and talk to your partner. Try to give an example of something else that slithers. Describe what slithering looks and feels like. Think about the opposite of slithering."

You might decide to do this for several other words in the book, perhaps collecting the words on index cards to add to a word wall or creating a small, impromptu chart of words to describe different ways to move.

DAY FOUR: Fluency

On this day, you'll focus on supporting fluency—especially pacing. Reading at an even pace is an important skill to practice. When young readers read too slowly, meaning can break down and understanding can be lost. On the other hand, when readers read too quickly they often miss important ideas and information, also compromising understanding. You might help your readers stabilize their reading rate by rereading a part that sounds too slow (or too quick). You also could use your pointer to scoop up the words, moving your readers to follow at an appropriate pace.

Today is a good time to begin drawing your students' attention to the punctuation marks on the page, teaching them how to read with different kinds of ending punctuation, quotation marks, and commas. Because this is the fourth read of the text, children will know where the tricky parts are, and you can coach them to be ready to read right through those parts.

Finally, you will want to you support your readers in using prosodic cues. Prosodic cues are all the meaning cues the author provides. You can have students study these cues, such as punctuation, font characteristics (italicized print, bold print, words printed in all capital letters, enlarged print), and even the tone of the text. Using every bit of information a text holds will allow students to read with increased expression and drama.

DAY FOUR FOCUS

✔ Read with fluency (appropriate pacing, parsing, and prosody).

✔ Draw attention to different types of punctuation.

✔ Read for meaning.

WARM UP

Reread one or two pages of a familiar text that contains dialogue to warm up voices for fluent reading.

Today you'll want to choose a familiar book that contains dialogue to read for your warm up—most likely a book you've already used in shared reading. Choose a few pages with particularly expressive dialogue. You might say to students, "We loved this book so much I thought we could read a few pages today to warm up our voices for reading *Tumbleweed Stew*. In fact, I've chosen a page where the characters are talking to help us remember what it feels like to talk just like the characters in the book." Then you might remind students of what happens in this particular part of the book and briefly read the pages, focusing on reading with expression. Quickly practicing with a known text will prepare students to do this work in *Tumbleweed Stew*.

FOURTH READING: *Tumbleweed Stew*

Reread the book, working on parsing (phrasing) to improve fluency.

"Readers, your voices are all nice and warm and ready to reread our book today. When you're reading along, should you read one word at a time, like a robot? No! You should scoop up the words and put them together to sound smooth. As we're reading today, if we notice that things are getting a little bit bumpy we'll reread so we can smooth it out. Here we go!"

Today you might choose to scoop your finger under the words as the kids read, dropping your voice but still providing a scaffold to help them read words with the appropriate phrasing.

Keep in mind the character's feelings, and think of what kind of voice you'll use.

In addition to thinking about phrasing, you'll want to coach students to use clues from the text to read dialogue with expression. For example, in the beginning of the story when Jack first encounters Longhorn you might pause students to think about how the characters are feeling before reading the dialogue. "Readers, I'm remembering that on this page Jack is trying to be really friendly to all the animals, but they aren't interested at all. In fact, they tell him to go away! Let's keep that in mind as we read this page and make sure our voices match how the characters are feeling!"

AFTER YOU READ

Draw students' attention to some of the "book language" in the text.

The language of stories is often more complex than our oral language, and as students read they encounter new phrases and sentence structures. Drawing their attention to these differences and practicing how new phrases go can be both helpful and fun.

Tumbleweed Stew provides lots of great opportunities for exploring book language, so today you might choose a few sentences or phrases to read together and notice the special language the author has chosen. For example, you might reread the page when Jack and Longhorn meet, asking children to listen closely for any phrases that sound like a book talking. Jack's introduction, "How do you do?" will probably catch their ears, and you could all have some fun thinking of the different ways we address new people, making connections between the children's oral language and the sentence structures of the book. Then you might find a few more places in the book to explore syntax, asking, "Readers, did anybody else notice some places where the book talks a little bit differently than we might?"

DAY FIVE: Putting It All Together

Today, the last day of this shared reading, you'll coach students to use all three cueing systems and everything they've learned this week to read with greater comprehension and fluency. The ability to orchestrate the reading process takes practice and hard work. Shared reading is a powerful vehicle for that work.

DAY FIVE FOCUS

✔ Read to orchestrate all three cueing systems and use everything you've learned all week.

WARM UP

Sing the "Be a Reading Boss!" song and read through your word solving chart to build confidence, excitement, and fluency.

You might start by celebrating all of the work students did in shared reading across the week, encouraging children to use *all* they know and to put it together to make this final read the very best. You might say, "We've worked on figuring out the hard words and making sure to check that they make sense, sound right, and look right. We made sure we read just like the characters' were feeling and scooped up our words to make our reading smooth. Let's put it *all* together to make this the very best read. Ready to show off everything you know? Go!"

FINAL READING: *Tumbleweed Stew*

Remind children that each time they reread, their voices become smoother and they understand the book even better. This is the message you want your children to carry with them back to their own independent reading. Read through the text fluently, then compliment the class on how their reading has improved in just one week of repeated practice.

AFTER YOU READ: Extend the Text

Celebrate the fun you've had reading the book all week. Make connections to the work students are doing as writers, and then use interactive writing to create a book review.

"Readers, what a great book that was. We had so much fun reading it all week, and now we know it so well. In fact, I was thinking it was such a good book, maybe we should write a review and recommend it to some of the other first-grade classrooms. They might want to read it too!"

As a class, brainstorm some reasons you liked the book and begin writing a letter together. If you're into the Grade 1 *Writing Reviews* unit of the Units of Study in Opinion, Information, and Narrative Writing, you might want to tuck in some of the strategies students are learning to use in their reviews to create an exemplar to use in writing workshop. You might want this work to carry into your interactive writing the next day. Your letter might say something like this:

Dear Class 1B,

We think the book *Tumbleweed Stew* is a great read!

One reason is that the story is really clever. Jack Rabbit tricks

the other animals into making a stew. It's also a fun

book to read because you can act out how

the characters move. For example, the snake slithers

and the deer trots. We even learned some new words.

Hope you enjoy the book!

From,

Class 1A

Of course, there are lots of other great ways to celebrate the book you've read and to extend comprehension. You could use interactive writing to support students' inferring skills by drawing speech or thought bubbles on different pages and inviting children to imagine what the characters are thinking in particular parts. For example, you might return to the first page and ask the children to consider what Jack Rabbit is thinking as he gets up to look at the sky, recording their ideas on the page.

If students are working on predicting, you might turn to the end of the story and invite them to imagine with you what might come next if the story were to continue, and then write that page together. Similarly, you might examine the text with an eye toward author's craft, finding places that you could embellish, perhaps by adding more descriptive language to bring the story to life or by revising the beginning to better grab readers' attention. For example, you could revisit a page in which the vegetables are being added to the stew and think of some fresh and inviting ways to describe each ingredient.

You might also choose to do some separate shared writing with your students to support language and writing development. You could do this by composing and recording a letter to the characters or to the author. You might even write your own class version of the story. You'll want to place copies of this shared or interactive writing in struggling students' book baggies so they can read these teacher-supported materials independently during reading workshop.

Additional opportunities to act out the story are a key way to deepen students' comprehension of texts and to support their language development. You might turn the text into a Reader's Theater activity, perhaps even providing materials for students to make simple props or puppets. They could then use these to act out the story as they turn the pages of the book. Finally, you might choose to have a grand discussion, digging more deeply into Jack's motivations for making tumbleweed stew or comparing and contrasting the book with *Stone Soup*.

As you end the week, find a special place in the classroom to store previous shared reading texts. Your students will want to read them again and again, returning to old favorites! Then choose another text and use this week's structure to plan for next week.